MATERIAL AND IDEOLOGICAL FACTORS IN INDIAN HISTORY

MATERIAL AND IDEOLOGICAL FACTORS IN INDIAN HISTORY

TARA CHAND

MANOHAR
2026

Due to the academic and scholarly importance of this volume, we are reprinting/republishing it from the original source without any modifications or changes. Therefore, some misprints and errors may occur.

First published 1966
Reprinted 2025, 2026
First eBook edition 2025

ISBN 978-93-6080-017-8 (hardbound)
ISBN 978-93-6080-209-7 (ebook)

Published by
Ajay Kumar Jain *for*
Manohar Publishers & Distributors
4753/23 Ansari Road, Daryaganj
New Delhi 110 002

Printed and bound in India

CONTENTS

FOREWORD

I have great pleasure in writing a FOREWORD to the Tagore Lectures delivered by Dr. Tara Chand in February last year. These lectures form part of the University Grants Commission's programme for the commemoration of the Centenary of our great poet Rabindra Nath Tagore. The Centenary was celebrated all over the world in 1961 and the Tagore Lectures, which will be held every alternate year in the University, have been supported by a substantial grant from the U.G.C.

Our first Tagore lecturer, Dr. Tara Chand, hardly needs any introduction to the academic world. Apart from being a scholar of international reputation and one of the foremost historians of India, he has achieved distinction in other fields also. He was Vice-Chancellor of the University of Allahabad and after Independence he was appointed as the Education Secretary in the Union Ministry of Education. Thereafter, he served as India's Ambassador in Iran and later as a member of the Rajya Sabha.

The theme of the lectures is of great interest. Dr. Tara Chand, with his wide sweep of history, has helped us in understanding the many forces which have moulded the life of the Indian people. He has made an important and original contribution to the study of the history of India.

I am happy that the Department of Medieval and Modern History has taken steps to publish Dr. Tara Chand's lectures.

University of Allahabad. R. K. NEHRU

INTRODUCTION

Tagore Lectures were delivered for the first time in February 1965. The academic council and the Faculty Board of Arts had passed a resolution during the Tagore Centenary year, recommending the establishment of a Tagore chair in the University. Earlier, recommendations to this effect had been conveyed to the University bodies by the University Grants Commission. This idea however did not materialise but as a result of a grant made by the above body the University proceeded to establish Tagore Lectures. These lectures are to be delivered every alternate year. A committee consisting of several heads of departments with the Vice-Chancellor as the President, select the Tagore lecturer of the year.

The centenary of the birth of poet Rabindra Nath Tagore roused great interest in the life and works of the poet. No literary figure of the East was so much worshipped and loved in his life time as Tagore was. His writings had brought solace to the war weary minds of the West. His work Gitanjali had become 'the best seller,' in 1913. His appeal was universal and the reason was, as he himself described, 'The same stream of life that runs through my veins night and day runs through the world and dances in rhythmic measures.'

Gandhi and Tagore together captured the imagination of the people not only in India but in many parts of the world. They together formed in the words of Prof. Tucci, 'the conscience of India in new ways.' If people in all parts of the world still fondly cherish the memory of the two great men, it is because of their faith in man. Having deeply read and imbibed the spirit of Indian culture, Tagore felt that the saviour with the divine message would arise on the Eastern horizon and give faith and strength to all who hear. It was in the fitness of things that Dr. B. Prasad then the Vice-Chancellor and members of the committee extended an invitation to Dr. Tara Chand, the eminent historian, who himself has such deep faith in Indian culture, to deliver the first Tagore Lectures. These lectures were held in the History department in February 1965 and the learned lecturer chose 'Material and Ideological factors in Indian History'.

Dr. Tara Chand M.A. (Alld.), D.Phil., (Oxon.) Member, Rajya Sabha, has been one of the most distinguished Indian Historians. He was born in 1888 and after his early education at Delhi and Meerut joined the Muir Central College, University of Allahabad, for his higher studies. He later went to Queens College, Oxford for a research degree in History. Dr. Tara Chand taught both History and Political Science for a number of years in the University of Allahabad and occupied the chair in Political Science after the demise of Dr. Beni Prasad D.Sc. He became the Vice-Chancellor of the University of Allahabad in 1947, and in the same year after India became independent he was offered the post of Secretary and Education Adviser in the Ministry of Education, Government of India. On retirement from the ministry in 1951 he became India's Ambassador in Iran Although not in active service, Dr. Tara Chand keeps himself busy in research work on Indian History. He became the President of Indian History Congress several years ago. He was known to Gandhiji and Pt. Jawahar Lal Nehru personally, who respected his views on various problems concerning the country. Dr. Tara Chand has many scholarly works to his credit. His research work 'Influence of Islam on Indian Culture' has gained very wide recognition. He is currently engaged in writing the History of the Freedom Movement of which one volume has already been published.

It was the privilege of the department of Medieval and

Modern History to hold the first Tagore Memorial lecture and to welcome one of the most distinguished alumni and teachers of the department.

The lectures are an illustration of the deep insight of Dr. Tara Chand in History. In the first lecture he has analysed the main features of the growth of Indian society and culture and has underlined the causes leading to the emergence of static economy and a rigid social system. Commenting on the lack of historical sense in Ancient India, Dr. Tara Chand feels that 'the transitoriness of the states during the formative period of literature was in all probability accountable for the lack of development of historical narrative. 'In the second lecture Dr. Tara Chand has emphasised the main aspects of the development of a spirit of co-operation and mutual adjustment existing between the Hindus and Muslims in the Medieval times. In the third lecture the learned lecturer has discussed the various aspects of Western impact on Indian life and culture and the reaction of the people to the new ideology of the West. From Ram Mohan Roy to Jawahar Lal Nehru was ushered in a remarkable age in India in which the contemporary Indian culture took shape.

The three lectures together enable us not only to grasp the significance of the contributions made in different periods by the leaders of thought but also of the factors responsible for promoting the syncretic attitude. It is in consonance with Tagore's views expressed in 'A Vision of India's History'. He wrote "But all the same I believe that we have cause to be proud of the fact that for a long series of centuries beset with vicissitudes of stupendous proportions, crowded with things that are incongruous and facts that are irrelevant, India still keeps alive the inner principle of her own civilisation against the cyclonic fury of contradictions and the gravitational pull of the dust".

History Department *O. P. Bhatnagar*

1

INDIA IN ANCIENT TIMES

I am greatly beholden to the Vice-Chancellor for extending to me the invitation to deliver the first series of Tagore Memorial Lectures. May I take the liberty to offer my congratulations to the Allahabad University on instituting these lectures to perpetuate the memory of Rabindra Nath Tagore, poet, philosopher, patriot and creator of modern India.

I propose in these lectures to review the history of India, not with the intention of presenting new facts, but in order to bring to the notice of the students of history a point of view which is slowly pervading the study, but which has not yet become established. This approach is not only preferable on academic grounds, it is worthy of consideration because it fulfils the needs of our country in its present predicament. I believe there is profound truth in Groce's statement, "all history is present history", and I must confess that in the writing of these lectures I have become more than ever before convinced of its relevance.

My first lecture deals with the ancient period, and the second with the Middle Ages; in the third lecture I have tried to discover in the long and meandering journey which India has traversed, the direction of India's march towards independence.

In all the three lectures my endeavour is to seek the meaning of the grand process whose beginnings can only be dimly perceived in the migration and settlement of the Aryans but which moves towards its finale through India's fight for freedom and its ultimate achievement.

So far Indian historians have been largely and rightly engaged in the discovery of facts and their endeavours have supplied us with much basic material which enables us to take a synoptic view of the forest of historical events without becoming wholly occupied with the multiplicity of the trees.

Of the three lectures the first suffers most from doubts regarding the identity of the trees and the paucity of their inventory. Ancient India is still the happy hunting ground for speculation. Much of the chronology is still quite uncertain and there remain wide gaps in our knowledge. The time sequence of cultural developments as we go back towards the remoter past becomes more and more indefinite. What happened during the long period of the efflorescence of Harappan culture is utterly unknown. It is conjectured that the Mohenjo-Daro and Harappan people and their cities were destroyed by the Aryan immigrants, a semi-nomadic folk, who in spite of their cultural backwardness were superior to their foes because they possessed better tools and weapons, horse drawn chariots and a language which indicated a high capacity for calculation, understanding and thought.

When did the Aryans come into India, what was the character of their migrations, where did they come from, are questions whose satisfactory answers are still unknown? Some even hold that they were not foreigners at all, but children of the Indian soil, who emigrated to western lands. But this theory remains unproved, at any rate, it is not acceptable to most historians. Then no dates are available to fix the time of their wanderings and settlements. So the long stretch of almost one thousand years remains without solid chronological pegs on which to hang the narrative of their movements. About the middle of the first millennium before Christ, a little feeble ray of light begins to penetrate into the darkness of the past.

From the birth of the Buddha to the death of Sankara is a period of nearly fifteen centuries, a period of historical chiaroscuro, of blazing light profusely illuminating the culture of India and of the penumbral obscurity spread over the field of politics and administration. It is a period of political vicissitudes—of the rise and fall of empires, of the waxing and waning of territorial kingdoms. During the period two empires flourished—the Mauryan and the Gupta—the first from 325 B.C. to 180 B C., and the second from 320 A.D. to the end of the fifth, and a number of regional principalities existed in different parts of India—in the Deccan the Satavahana, the Chalukya, the Pallava, the Chola; and in the North the Vardhamana of Kanauj. Three centuries followed during which most of northern India was dominated by Rajput dynasties and the Deccan by the Rashtrakutas. The South was held in fee under the sway of the great Cholas.

With the turn of the eleventh century the curtain begins to descend upon the long period of ancient history. New forces begin their play and profound changes occur in society, politics and culture. The scene shifts, the Middle Age of India sets in, new faces, new families and new races appear upon the stage. Life is more chequered, its sound and colour more variegated. During its latter half the wealth and splendour of the Mughal empire are so fascinating as to draw men from far off lands, attracted by the wonder that was Ind.

From the eighth century of the Christian era, the writer of Indian history finds new material with which to eke out the exiguous information supplied by the Indian actors who occupied the stage. India comes into contact with a restless, dynamic, inquisitive culture, from whose bases in Medina, Baghdad, Damascus, Arab travellers, scientists, merchants and missionaries, Ulama and Sufis, poured out in an unending stream to visit India and record what they saw or heard. Their accounts give a note of solid certainty to the political facts of the times.

When in the eleventh century A.D. the Muslim Turks occupied the Punjab the chronicles written by Persian scholars become available and as time passes their volume increases, and although one cannot complain of **le' embarras des richesses,** nevertheless, the material is adequate for a full and systematic narrative of political events. For these times apart from Persian chronicles, histories written in Sanskrit and records maintained in Indian languages are also at the disposal of the enquirer. Thus from the eighth to the eighteenth century, unlike the preceding period, factual guidance is plentiful. There is no more groping in the dark, thanks to the writers whose sense of history, although very different from that of the moderns, illumines the scene with a light which was unknown before.

With the conquest of India by the British, we enter upon a period of documents and records in great profusion—authentic state papers of governments and of many non-officials who took part in the affairs of the times. We have also newspapers, reports, memoirs, autobiographies and printed books. In fact, no dearth of material for history!

Each one of these three periods presents its own difficulties to the student: the first, because of the scantiness of reliable information and almost complete absence of historical treatises; the second, because of the peculiar bias of the chroniclers who narrate the deeds of the rulers but keep silent about the activities of the ruled; the third, because of the difference in points of view and lines of approach.

It is an amazing fact that so far as the first period is occupied the Punjab the chronicles written by Persian scholars of the eighteenth century, for with the exception of some myths and legends the entire past was shrouded in Cimmerian darkness. Not a single certain and reliable date of a king or priest, of an event or a text, was known. This is peculiarly surprising, for unlike other ancient countries, India has enjoyed a rare continuity of culture over a time span of almost five thousand years. From the protohistoric Harappan past to the present there is scarcely a break in this long and eventful history, so much so that much of the culture of the past is still living today. Yet, no author of the first four thousand years has left to us any systematic account of those four millennia.

Many explanations have been given for this, lack of historical sense, indifference to worldly affairs, occupation with the mystical, the spiritual, and the changeless, and apathy towards the impermanent, ever changing and sensuous. But the curious fact remains that in the vast ocean of Indian literary output covering almost every conceivable branch of knowledge only history is absent.

Our surprise becomes greater when it is realised that it could not be due to lack of basic material. Sutas and Magadhas, Vandins or Stavakas preserved genealogies of kings, rishis, and traditions of great men, which were the sources of information for **Ithihasa** and **Purana**. At the courts of kings careful records of important happenings were kept which is attested by inscriptions, **Dana patras,** biographical poems and dramas, the direct testimony of travellers like Hiuen Tsiang, the monumental historical work of Kalhana, and the existence of an official at court—the **Akshpatal-adhikrita.**

Perhaps the explanation may be sought in the fact that history in the sense of narrative is dependent upon history in the sense of event. In the second sense ancient Indian political history is peculiarly particularistic, spasmodic, discontinuous both in space and time.

Protohistoric times are too primitive for any historical writing. Early Vedic age was a period of settlement of pastoral tribes in the lands watered by the seven rivers from the Indus to the Sarasvati. The later Vedic age—the age of Yajur and Atharva, of the Brahmanas, Aranyakas and Upanishads, is a period of movement, expansion, and of strain and stress—a second age of settlements to the east and south of the Punjab. During this age the region of the exploits of the early Aryans falls into obscurity, new geographical environment, new groups, new social conditions, new ideologies, new economic systems and political organisations appear. All history is reflection on the past, but reflection requires a period of rest and stability. But both were unknown in the kaleidoscopic changes of the times.

A fresh period in political history begins with the foundation of Haryanka dynasty in Magadha. But the account of the dynasties—Haryanka, Saisunaga and Nanda, which preceded the accession of the Mauryas to power, is so confused and the history so full of vicissitudes and violent deeds as to leave no room for settled and peaceful progress. The Mauryas built up remarkably quickly a vast empire, but it seems to have declined equally fast. Within twenty six years of Asoka's death the country was again subject to Greek attacks. The Sungas and Kanvas ruled over a shrivelled empire undergoing pangs of dissolution at the hands of internal rebellious chiefs and governors and foreign invaders—the Yavanas from Bactria. The curtain falls on Magadha and for the next three centuries and a half the country has no history.

When the curtain lifts again on the rise of the Guptas Magadha has a second period of glory. Unfortunately, it did not last even one hundred years. The Empire began to totter under Kumara Gupta and after a short recovery under Skanda, declined steadily under the blows of the Hunas.

After the Guptas no Hindu empire of similar dimensions was established and a multiplicity of centres of political power in different parts of northern India rose and fell. The dynasties which ruled at these centres were usually short-lived. In the Deccan and the South, however, a number of ruling houses retained kingship within the family for long periods, from two to four hundred years.

Thus the state which provides the subject matter of history and society which is the bearer and maintainer of the state were lacking in universality and stability in India. The absence of a universal Indian society is attested by among others the fact that there was no common designation for the people of India, till foreigners gave them the appellation of Hindu. The multiplicity of societies and states, mutually at feud, greedy to extend their sway over their neighbours, their short-lived triumphs in building up empires succeeded by long intervals of anarchy were conditions quite uncongenial for historical compositions.

The transitoriness of the states during the formative period of literature was in all probability accountable for the lack of development of historical narrative. While the basic material was not lacking the scholarship competent to produce this type of literature received little encouragement; for instance, the Sutas and Magadhas were demoted from their early social status to the position of inferior castes—charioteer and musician. The Kayasthas who were Brahmans in Kalhana's **Rajataringini** and held offices of the Prime Minister of the realm and the Commander-in-Chief of the army, and in fact all the administrative posts, were in later ages treated as clerks and writers far below the Brahmans.

All literary effort, unfortunately, tended to concentrate in the hands of the Brahmans, with the result that exaggerated emphasis was laid on the religious and other worldly aspects of life, so much so that even sciences—physical and social, were regarded as appendages of religion. Unprecedented devotion was poured over religious literature so that almost the entire output of the Indian mind was overshadowed by it. There is no literature of any people so deeply coloured with religion, nor any so voluminous. The impulse given in early years to the intellectual movement made it difficult for writers in later ages to abandon the paths carved out by tradition and to venture upon new lines. Thus it was that **Ithihasa** and **Purana** which had the capability of blossoming into history grew into encyclopaedic works on ethics, philosophy, theology, cosmogony, eschatology, etc.

The stories about the authors of the Ramayana and the Mahabharata—the two great **Itihasas,** and the compilers of the **Puranas** allude to this confusion regarding their status. Valmiki was originally a bandit, a Robinhood, who plundered travellers but was later reformed and then became the singer of the good deeds of Rama. Vyasa Krishnadvaipayana, of dark complexion, son of the maiden Satyavati and the physical begetter of the Pandavas, Dhritarashtra, Vidura, was the famed author of the **Mahabharata.** These strange legends raise questions about the character of the great works, the status of the writers, and the social manners of the times, which are difficult to answer.

The **Puranas** which were in all likelihood only **Vanshavalis** (genealogies) and stories about kings maintained and recited by the Sutas were taken over by the legendary Brahman Lomaharsana, his son Ugrasravas, and his disciples. It was made a part of the vedic canon—**Purana Veda,** and attributed to Veda Vyasa.

In the face of such staggering uncertainty and obscurity and with blanks in the past extending sometimes over centuries to rationalise the history of ancient India, is a hazardous adventure. Only the belief that the affairs of man alone cannot be a disorderly and meaningless pullulation of accidents in the midst of the vast orderly universe—which would be wholly incomprehensible if it was not orderly, and whose understanding by the human mind would be quite inexplicable unless, after making all the allowances, the mind was not an organ of rational order, sustains the historian in his endeavour to unravel the significance of the vague but enormous movements which have unfortunately not found a written record. So historians have speculated to discover the why and how of historical developments, and may be their historical imagination is gradually succeeding in extracting from the known facts the linkages which give unity and continuity to the process of history.

History in India which began with the Harappan civilisation possesses a remarkable continuity, for each phase of this history carries within it much of the preceding phase, so that the sequence of cultures is never broken, and India's individuality is indelibly impressed upon all its phases. This is a remarkable phenomenon which India shares only with one other country, namely, China. It is only partly explained by the geography of India, for although mountains and oceans which surround the country on all sides seemingly isolate it from the world, India has had throughout its history very close relations with its neighbours—both across the land frontiers as well as beyond the seas. In fact, surprisingly a great deal of our information comes from what the foreigners have said about India. This is particularly true of protohistoric and ancient periods of our history.

We may then start our enquiry about the character of our history with the first civilisation that appeared upon the soil of India, namely, the Harappan, which seems to have spread at one time not only in the valleys of the Indus and its tributaries, but into the western region of Rajasthan, Kathiawar and Gujarat and also possibly in the Gangetic plain.

The important features of this culture were that it was urban, with burnt brick buildings, waterworks and drainage. It was bourgeois, interested in agriculture, industry and commerce rather than war and conquest. Its class system indicates a probable division into four sections corresponding to the four Varnas of the Hindus, but among the higher classes there was not much difference of wealth. Extremes of luxury and riches which are an appanage of a militaristic aristocratic society seemed to be absent. The economic basis was agrarian, sandy soil of the Punjab and Sindh and the adequate rainfall of those times yielded to the Harappan cultivator with his simple tools—the many pronged harrow drawn by bullocks, with the control of irrigation by dams—an abundance of crops. In religion the cult of Siva as Pasupata, and Sakti or mother goddess, was prevalent. With Siva was associated the practice of Yoga as well as the worship of phallus; both were practised; so also lustration in the rivers, wells and tanks. Among animals the bull and among trees the **Pipal** were held sacred.

The society was static. No radical change is perceptible in its history of nearly 1500 years. The same cult, almost the same social stratification, the same style of architecture, arts and pottery, an identical system of weights and measures and an identical script continue from the beginning to the end.

Evidently these peaceful peoples had farflung commercial contacts, by land as well as by sea. Their seals, articles and art motifs have been found in many ancient sites in West Asia and Egypt—for example, in the Ur of the Sumerians, in a pre-Sargonid inscription in cuneiform of about 2500 B.C., at Kish, Tell Amarna, and other places in Mesopotamia; in Susa of the Elamites; in Dilmun the island of Bahrein in the Persian Gulf—steatite seals and copper. The Assyrians imported from India copper, ivory, monkeys and pearls, besides cotton cloth. A vase has been found at Tell Arab with the Indus humped bull.

On the other hand, Harappan sites have provided objects made in the West Asian lands. Indians imported silver besides other metals and precious stones like turquoise and lapis lazuli. The Gilgamesh legend of a man holding two standing tigers at bay is repeated in a Harappan seal, and the bull with the elephant head—evidently an imitation of the copper plate of the Harappa art, in Jemdat Nasr (Mesopotamia).

The unwarlike Harappans who built citadels within the city walls for defence, had little experience of war and combat. Although Mohenjo-Daro was built nine times there is no evidence of violent change except in the last stage. Their weapons were not made for execution, the copper spearheads were too soft, the blades flat and easily bent and axe heads without holes for the shafts. They owned asses but had no horses to ride on to battle. When, therefore, the warlike semi-nomadic Aryans descended upon them in their horse drawn chariots, invoking the battle god Indra intoxicated with wine and armed with the thunderbolt, they carried fire and sword amidst the gentle and industrious Harappans–designated them as Dasas and Dasyus, burnt their towns, slaughtered their men and played havoc with their irrigation dams by releasing the waters and destroying the fields.

What happened to these first Indians, these lovers of peace and religion? They seemed to be non-political in the mass, and devoted largely to economic pursuits and a life of comparative comfort, worshipping gods and goddesses which did not inspire terror or fear and did not require bloody sacrifices to appease them. Apparently the rank and file were either annihilated or absorbed by the conquerors as an inferior section of the Aryan tribes or forced to take refuge in hills and forests far from the Aryan habitations. But among their higher ranks some must have found a place of equal status among the Aryans. Their kings are mentioned in the **Rgveda**, for instance, Sambara who fought Divodasa, and Bheda who led the Ajas, Singrus and Yakshas living on the banks of the Jumna and gave battle to Sudas the hero of the Dasarajna–the war of the ten Kings on the Parushni (Ravi). Again Dasa kings whose names were Balbutha and Taruksa are praised by Vasa Asvya a Brahman priest for their generosity. The Aryan chiefs entered into alliances and made treaties with the Dasa kings.

It is not easy to determine the race or language of these inhabitants of Harappa and Mohenjo-Daro. The Brahui language which is still spoken in a part of this region belongs to the Dravidian family. Dravidian words found in western languages and in Greek and Latin must have travelled with the exports sent from Indian ports, for example, the Tamil 'arisi' (rice) is the Greek Oryze, and Tamil Togei Greek Taos (peacock). King Solomon obtained from India ivory and its name **ibha** (elephant), monkeys with their designation Kapi or Kophi (Hebrew), peacocks which were called Tukki after Tamil Togei. King Hiram of Tyre received gold, precious stones and sandal from Ophir, that is, Supara. Indian emeralds (marakat) were known in the west as Smaragdus, Vaiduryas as byrullas (beryl), pippilli (pepper) as Papperi, Sarkara (sugar) as Kakhhrow, Karpasa (cotton) as Karpasos, and Sringvera (ginger) as Zingiberis.

It is surmised from facts like these that the Harappans were Dravidians who had migrated from some region in the west in prehistoric times, in times contemporary with the early Egyptian dynasties, and kingdoms of Sumer, Akkad and Elam. They established an urban culture in India.

The Aryans were a mixture of races speaking Indo-European languages and leading a pastoral life somewhere in the vast tracts between the Tien Shan and the Caucasus. In the third millennium before Christ, for reasons not well known, these semi-nomadic tribes began to move east and west. The tradition is that five principal Aryan tribes (**pancha janah**) migrated to India—Puru, Yadu, Turvasa, Anu and Druhyu. With them others also came, e.g., Tritsus and Bharatas. They settled down in various parts of the country called Saptasindhavah—between the Indus, its five tributaries and the Sarasvati, where they remained during the time of the compilation of the **Rgveda.**

It is necessary to know what kind of people they were on their arrival in India and what changes overtook them during the period of their settlements and expansion towards the eastern and southern regions of India.

Contrary to popular and pious views prevalent among some sections of our countrymen, our Aryan forbears do not appear to have been a very ascetical or other worldly or even inward looking peoples. Less advanced in many branches of material culture, they had to learn lessons in matters of worship and training of the mind from their foes whom they conquered and subjugated. The fact is the Aryans were completely transformed under the influence of the pre-Aryan peoples.

The picture of the Aryans depicted in Rgveda shows them to be a full-blooded, semi-civilised, illiterate, agrarian folk leading a simple village life. Their chief occupations were two—fighting and sacrificing, and the object of both was success in this world and a comfortable, pleasurable life in the world to come. The historical portions of the Vedas are filled with accounts of wars and campaigns—of victories over the Aryans and non-Aryans and of fights between one Aryan tribe against another and paeans of glory to celebrate these triumphs. Here is a song to secure victory in battle:

> The warrior's look is like a thunderous rain-cloud's, when, armed with mail, he seeks the lap of battle.
>
> Be thou victorious with unwounded body: so let the thickness of thy mail protect thee.
>
> With Bow let us win kine, with Bow the battle, with Bow be victors in our hot encounters.
>
> The Bow brings grief and sorrow to the foeman: armed with the Bow may we subdue all regions.
>
> Close to his car, as fain to speak, She presses, holding her well-loved Friend in her embraces.
>
> Strained on the Bow, She whispers like a woman—this Bow-string that preserves us in the combat.[1]
>
> The priest's praise of a patron brings out his unabashed greed for goods of this earth. It reads thus:
>
> A hundred necklets from the King, beseeching, a hundred gift-steeds I at once accepted;
>
> Of the lord's cows a thousand, I Kakshivan. His deathless glory hath he spread to heaven.

---

1 GRIFFITH, Ralph T.H.: *THE MYMNS OF THE RIGVEDA*, vol. 1 (Benaras, 1896), pp. 645-46.

Horses of dusky colour stood beside me, ten chariots,
Svanaya's gift, with mares to draw them.

Kine numbering sixty thousand followed after. Kakshivan
gained them when the days were closing.

Forty bay horses of the ten cars' master before a
thousand lead the long procession.

Reeling in joy Kakshivan's sons and Pajra's have
groomed the coursers decked with pearly trappings.[1]

Sacrifice was the central rite of the Aryan religion. Philosophically it was symbolic of the great act of Cosmic creation, an invocation to the divine power to aid the sacrificer in his identification with the universal order, the process of evolution and involution. The sacrifice transformed the human agent, but equally compelled the gods, for all were bound together in the chain of **Rta**—the principle of law which operated in the universe and in man. It is for the sake of sacrifice that the hymns were made and collected in the **Rgveda.** The **Sama** arranged them for the purpose of chanting at sacrifices, the **Yajur** guided the priest in the details of the ritual, the Brahmans explained the sacrifices and the Srauta Sutras described them in their parts.

These functions determined the organisation of society. It is clear that the Vedic Aryans did not constitute a single social or political unit. The tribes were many and they lived and acted as separate communities. Each tribe was an organic whole in itself. Each had its own parts and they were not common with others. The parts were divided functionally but not hereditarily in the beginning. Some families of the tribe were specially marked out for political leadership. They were **Rajanva,** or Kshatriyas. Others specialised in the performance of sacrifices and making and chanting of hymns, the **Brahmans.** But there was no rigid distinction between them. Among the

[1] *Ibid.*, p. 174.

Vedic rishis, the seers, we find Brahmans of course, but also Kshatriya kings and even Vaisyas. Visvamitra, the five sons of Vrisagir the Rajarshi, and Devapi the brother of Santanu were Kshatriya hymn makers. Nabhanedishtha rishi was a Vaisya.

According to the **Matsya Purana,** Manu Vaivasvata, Ida and Pururavas the Kshatriyas were utterers of hymns, so were Bhalana, Vandya and Sanskirthi the Vaisyas.[1]

The third and the major part of the tribe consisted of the Vaisyas. In fact, Visa was the tribe, of which the Rajanya and the Brahman were the privileged sections. The Vaisyas were not only cattle breeders and agriculturists, but also practitioners of other crafts. But there was no caste divisions among them yet. Risi Angirasa says:

> A bard am I, my dad's a leech, mummy lays corn upon the stones.
>
> Striving for wealth, with varied plans, we follow our desires like kine. Flow, Indu, flow for Indra's sake.[2]

Even later books like the **Mahabharata** and the **Puranas** which embody ancient traditions make all the castes as descended from one progenitor, viz., Manu. According to the **Vaua Purana,** "The son of Gritsmada was Sunaka, from whom sprung Saunaka. In his family were born Brahmans, Kshatriyas, Vaisyas and Sudras, twice born men with various functions."

These texts make it obvious that the caste system was a late development. It had no sanction in the **Rgveda.** How it arose and was recognised when established and not created by the **Smritis** is another story. In any case caste has no basis in Vedic religion. Its appearance was the result of sociological and economic causes which came into operation later.

The end of the Vedic age was due to a number of causes. Apparently the wandering Aryans were temporary sojourners in the lands of the Saptasindhavah. For how long each tribe

1 Muir, *Sanskrit Texts,* 1, 279.
2 GRIFFITH, op. cit., vol. II (Benares, 1897), p. 380.

continued to occupy the territory, on which it had settled originally, cannot be ascertained. But the region through which the river Sarasvati and Drisadavati flowed was the sacred homeland where the **Rgveda** hymns were arranged and this may have taken many centuries. During the period many wars were fought among the Aryan tribes, the most devastating of them being the **Mahabharata.** Then some of the old tribes disappeared and new ones emerged into prominence.

It is also likely that the natural growth of the human and cattle population of the pastoral Aryans and especially the multiplication of ruling families rendered the Punjab unable to support them and compelled them to seek new lands for settlement elsewhere. The ownership of landed property which was vested in the tribe and was administered by the King may also have prompted the younger members of the ruling families to migrate.

So they moved east and south. This movement did not involve the transfer of whole tribes, but the ruling families and their priests. The Kurus moved into Panchala, Aikshvakus into Kosala and Ayodhya. Later Videh, Vaisali, Magadha and Anga were occupied. The Vidarbhas accompanied with Agastya moved south, and the Haihayas now divided into five branches into Central India, Malwa and Gujarat.

With the expansion of the geographical horizon a new era of history began. The first important change was demographic, the settlers small in numbers were warriors and priests and their subjects were mostly local inhabitants or a mixed group of the old Vaisyas and the local people. There was also a large accession of the fourth class the Sudras mainly cultivators and artisans. Their economy also changed. Pastoral pursuits began to lose their importance and agrarian occupations became more important. Agriculture assured greater stability to society which became more stationary and static. The eastern regions were cleared of forests by burning them because axes and other tools made of iron for felling trees were in short supply. But the virgin soil with abundance of rains and multiplicity of rivers yielded bumper crops.

In the east Magadha was endowed with metals, accessible encrustations of iron on the Barabar hills and deposits of copper and iron in Dhalbhum and Singhbhum districts. Iron provided better and more efficient tools to artisans, and the ploughs replaced the harrow. Industrial and agricultural produce increased. The military class acquired weapons which gave them irresistible superiority over the masses, now consisting largely of dark men of indigenous races.

The immediate results were many. Socially, the differentiation between the higher and the lower classes which was associated with their skin pigmentation became rigid and so function became stratified into caste. This tendency affected the higher class too. The sacrifices prescribed in the Vedas were grand public rites, **Asvamedha, Vajpeyá**, elaborate, prolonged, requiring the services of many priests and extensive arrangements. With the passage of time they became more complex and as they demanded extreme precision in chanting the accompanying hymns and performing the elaborate rites, the priests had perforce to become professional hierophants. At the same time the warriors engaged in constant wars became hereditary fighting caste. Thus the three upper castes and the fourth lower caste came into being.

Marriage laws also altered; strict rules of endogamy and exogamy were established. At first both **anuloma** and **pratiloma** alliances were allowed, then the marriage of a lower class male with the higher class female was forbidden, and still later even **anuloma** marriages were frowned upon, although they never ceased completely. So late as 1922 and 1931, the Bombay High Court declared them valid.

The other Vedic occupations also hardened into castes and were accommodated in the system of the four classes. As society developed in the eastern regions large surpluses of agricultural produce accrued, crafts flourished, and trade expanded. Trade was stimulated by the opening up of the country from north to south and east to west. In the time of the Buddha the following trade routes are mentioned, from Tamralipti, by way of Champa, Pataliputra, Benaras, Kausambi, Vidisa, Ujjayini to Bhrgu-Kachha; from Kausambi to Mathura, then via Rajasthan to the mouth of the Indus, or from Mathura to Delhi, then across the Punjab to Taxila, then Kabul and from there to Central Asia or to Meshed and the Caspian coast. The road to the South proceeded from Ujjayini to Pratishthana and then passed over the Deccan plateau and the Krishna rivers to Kanchi and to Madura.

Another factor in the growth of trade was greater accessibility and growing opportunities of contacts with foreign lands. The protohistoric trade routes over land may have been closed during the migration of the Aryan tribes—the Kassites, the Hittites, the Mitannis, the Urartians, etc., into Iran, Asia Minor and Mesopotamia. But with the rise of the Assyrian empire in north Mesopotamia in the tenth century B.C., and especially its expansion under the Sargonid rulers after the middle of the eighth century B.C., and their successors the Chaldaeans of Babylon and the Achaemenids of Iran during the seventh century B.C., the old trade through the Persian Gulf revived and expanded. Indian goods travelled over land when the Achaemenid empire restored contacts between India and the West, but in larger quantity by sea to the Mediterranean world—Egypt, the Fertile Crescent and Greece, by way of Persian Gulf and the Red Sea and then across Mesopotamia to the Mediterranean coast, to Coptos on the Nile and down the river to its mouth, or from Berenice on the coast of the Red Sea. It looks as if command over these routes was an important factor in the rise and fall of the kingdoms in western Asia—Assyria, Chaldaea and Iran. Sea borne traffic went eastwards, too, to Malaya, Indonesia and China from the ports of Bengal—Tamluk, and from the Cholamandaia.

The evolution of the Indian scripts—Brahmi and Kharoshti in these times, undoubtedly under the influence of Accadian and Aramaic, show the plenitude of the intercourse. A later evidence is the Baveru Jataka probably composed in the fourth century B.C., but referring to earlier times.

All these circumstances point to and explain the ascendancy of Magadha in Indian history from the seventh century before Christ to the seventh century A.D. when this region remained the political hub and the social centre of India. The two great empires of this period—the Maurya and the Gupta, had their geographical base here, and the two great religions—Buddhism and Jainism commenced their career in this land. This region supplied the economic foundations of political power—agrarian products and plenty of raw materials of industry. The growth of economic life is attested by the spread of institutions like contract, mortgage, interest, usury, and increase of coinage—of which the hoards of punch marked coins are a witness, and monetary exchange in place of barter. Real property of private individuals in houses and gardens—although not in cultivated fields yet, had come into existence.

Magadhan economy brought prosperity. Growth of wealth led to the proliferation of arts and crafts and a sudden extension of a rich corporate life, with a well developed and well organised guild system of merchants and craftsmen. The story of Anathapindaka the merchant who purchased for a Buddhist monastery the Jetvana by covering the garden with coins of gold is indicative of the richness that prevailed.

So far as society was concerned the evidence of the Smritis and Panini's Grammar which were in all likelihood compiled in this period, is to the effect that the old tribalism was breaking down, the fourfold division of each tribe designated by the term **Varna** was giving way to the multiplicity of the caste system or **jati.** The castes were subdivided on the basis of locality, e.g., Avanti Brahmana, Surashtra Brahman, who were the precursors of the latter-day Malawi, Sarasvata, Maharashtri, Gurjara and other Brahmans; Punchala, Darada, Yaudheya, and other Kshatriyas. The Vaishyas and Sudras were divided in accordance with occupation. So far as the Vaisyas were concerned their status had been lowered in spite of the fact that originally they were full Aryans. They were hardly distinguished from the Sudras. According to the **Aitreya-Brahman** they were described as payers of tribute, "to be oppressed at will". Manu regarded their function to be cattle breeding. But during this period of Magadhan ascendancy their importance had risen considerably and they exercised much influence.

The Sudras remained on the whole inferior members of society. They were the food producers and menial servitors, who had no ownership rights in land, but paid a part of the produce as tribute to the state. Below them came the outcastes, the untouchables, the Nishadhas and Chandalas.

But even though tribalism receded, the concept of a universal Indian society did not emerge. In the seventh century B.C. there were sixteen Janpadas or independent states jealous of one another and often at war among themselves. Some of the Vedic tribes were already extinct, others began to disappear as Magadha acquired greater power. Videh of the Ikshavakus was gone, Anga had become part of Magadha, Kasi was annexed to Kosala, and Kosala was occupied by Ajatsatru, who also conquered the Lichhavis and the Mallas. His son destroyed the Sakyas. The Nandas conquered Kuru Panchala, and the process culminated in the conquest of the whole of India from Kabul to Kaveri by the Mauryas.

The state which the Mauryas established was a highly complex organisation. In its activities the priest played an insignificant part. Many Kshatriyas had become tribeless mercenaries. They were employed in vast numbers in the imperial armies. According to classical accounts the Nandas had an army consisting of 20,000 cavalry, 2,000 chariots, 200,000 footmen and a large number of elephants—between three to six thousand. Plutarch estimated Chandragupta's army at 600,000, and Megasthenes reported 400,000 men in a single camp of his.

The fighters were less dependent on horse chariots, because possibly good horses were now not easily available from

Central Asia or Persia; but elephants had been domesticated and trained for both peaceful and warlike purposes, and the elephant force was irresistible in the India of those days. The monarchy was thus raised to great heights of power. But the expensive army and the elaborate system of administration could not be sustained without increasing state revenues, and consequently pressure on payers of land revenue grew and the middle class tax payers received great attention.

The Artha Sastra's recommendations for raising the revenues shows the tremendous pressure on state finances. Apart from capital levies on cultivators, special contributions from merchants, half the earnings of actors and prostitutes were mulcted and the entire property of goldsmiths confiscated. The other items suggested were sale of titles and insignia, spoliation of temples and monasteries and a number of fraudulent transactions—all which sounds very familiar in 1965.

How was the Maurya administrative system organised? The hierarchy of the executive officers consisted of upraja, yuvaraja, kumara, or the viceroys of the king; Pradesikas or provincial governors; district and departmental officials—Rajukas, Yutas, Mahamatras and Adhyaksas; city officers; Nagaraka or Purapala (which later became Kotwal); and village officers—Gramabhojaka or Gramani. The multiplicity of officials looking after the material and moral well being of the people gives the impression of modern governmental methods. But the reality was different. Distances were great, means of transport and communication slow. The army could hardly move two **yojanas** or about 10 miles in 24 hours. Much therefore must have been left to local discretion, which is borne out by the fact that the tendency to defy and rebel against the central authority was constant. The result was that India never developed like China, a bureaucracy which in spite of dynastic revolutions and foreign conquests could maintain the continuity of the state intact.

Then in spite of the appearance of the grandeur of the imperial court, the high sounding titles of the imperial officials and the lavish display of pomp and magnificence of regal appointments, it has to be recognised that in substance governmental powers were limited. Laws which were applicable to personal matters, to caste and class were beyond state jurisdiction. In cases of personal law the priests—Brahmanas and Sramanas, were masters. The affairs of caste and corporation were the concern of their own committees or **Panchayats.** The corporations were known to maintain their own troops. The villages were autonomous. Law and justice—except criminal causes and treason, were largely in the keeping of society itself, which regarded the King as an agent, whose duty was to protect the people and their Dharma.

The Maurya empire presented an imposing facade but internally it was a rickety political structure. It sprawled over the greater part of India, but there was no cohesion and unity among its multiracial and multilingual subjects. It was neither a unitary nor a federal state, but a loose confederation of provinces, principalities protectorates, dependencies and tribal territories. It was autocratic but bound by traditions and religious regulations. It had no means and institutions to insure perpetuity. Its horizontal structure ignored the principle of balance and check and aided and encouraged particularism.

These inherent weaknesses were aggravated by the economic imbalance which was perhaps inevitable. A farflung empire with its frontiers threatened by the strong neighbours and internal peace and order menaced by refractory elements within needed military forces, which entailed expenditure on a large scale. To meet this expenditure taxation had to be maintained at a high level. Religion and force had to be employed to prevent discontent from assuming dangerous proportions.

That Mauryan economy was fully extended and over strained is evident from Artha Sastra's provisions for raising revenue. Other evidence is furnished by the debased coinage. It is also possible that disturbed conditions in Central and Western Asia affected northern India's overland trade and gave a blow to its economic prosperity. The Seleucid empire which succeeded Alexander's conquest in Asia began to disintegrate. The Parthians and Bactrians divided its provinces in the east. The Bactrians or the Indo-Greek (Yavanas) attacked the Mauryan empire in the second century B.C. and took possession of the western region from Kabul to Kachh cutting off the overland relations of India with western countries. Then the period of five and a half centuries after Alexander's conquest in 323 B.C. and the rise of the Sasanians in 224 A.D. was one of conflict and instability in West Asia—wars between the Seleucids, the Romans and the Parthians. Mesopotamia became the scene of struggles and soon the Arabs marched in, which interfered with the trade between the Persian Gulf and the Mediterranean coast, for the security of the route of the caravans was no longer guaranteed.

From the sudden and catastrophic fall of the Mauryan to the foundation of the Gupta empire is an interval of nearly five hundred years. For northern India it was a period of great turmoil. The crumbling of the authority of the Magadhan empire weakened the bonds which had kept the principalities and tribal chieftancies together and political enfeeblement encouraged the invasions of the foreigners who established their dominion in the northwestern region. Kanishka, the Kushana, occupied the country from Afganistan to Bihar. Opportunity was seized by the Satavahanas of the Deccan to create a barrier between the north and the south. So that although the trade of the Dravida lands with both the west and the east flourished, the north did not receive equal benefit from it. Of this trade the goal was the Roman Empire during the first four centuries of the Christian era. It was routed from the ports on the Malabar and Coromandel coasts—from Musiri (Malabar), Korkai (Pandya territory), Kaveripattnam (on the mouth of the river), through the Indian Ocean and the Red Sea—Socotra, Berenice, Coptos, Alexandria, then Rhodes to Italy. In exchange for its spices, perfumes, jewellery, textiles, ivory, iron, dyes, foodstuffs (sugar, rice and ghee), animals and birds, India received from Rome mainly gold—bullion and specie. Pliny's complaint is well known; extravagant and degenerate habits of the Romans caused a drain to the East of 100 (or 500) million sesterces a year.

Was it Roman gold which helped the Satavahanas to build an empire from coast to coast?

The fall of the Roman Empire was fortunately compensated by the rise of the Sasanian empire, which established a vast area of peace from Oxus and the Indus in the east to the Euphrates and Arabian coast on the west. From the third to the eight century A.D. the Iranians and the Arabs carried on an extensive commerce with India and with countries of the far east. Both the overland routes and the sea lanes were open again for the merchants trading between the east and the west. Both Southern India and the North profited by the resumption of trade.

In the South the Chalukyas, the Pallavas, and then the Cholas acquired power and built up extensive dominions in India and outside—Ceylon and Southeast Asia. In the north the Gupta empire revived the glories of the Mauryas. The period of efflorescence of both coincided with the resumption of trade with the outside countries.

During the half a millennium following the fall of the Mauryan empire, northern India was a welter of contending forces, confusion and foreign rule. Naturally society and culture underwent changes of a far-reaching character in these years.

So far as the economic life was concerned there was an evident setback. The abundance and prosperity of the Mauryan age, its profitable agricultural and industrial pursuits, exploitation of mineral resources, growth of flourishing towns and cities, are no more. The impulse derived from the migration and settlement of the man pushing forward the frontiers eastwards and southwards and experimenting with fresh opportunities of developing the soil and metal industries were exhausted. The stimulus of expanding trade, internal and external, had received a check.

Life tended to become stagnant and stereotyped. A static economy and a rigid social system embraced society in its grip. They obstructed the formation of large communities and states. Political or social organisation on a broad countrywide scale became impossible.

Political insecurity affected the life of the villages. They became self-sufficient producers of food and other consumable articles. With their surplus they purchased the few commodities which the village could not itself supply—salt and metals being the most important. They grew into autonomous units, making arrangements for the regulation of their communal life through village and caste panchayats and officials like headman. They employed their own police (**chowkidar**), their own judiciary (**Sastri**), and the Brahaman who was both the teacher and the priest. The village had its own servants and maintained its own hereditary artisans, and it celebrated its own festivals, public rites and entertainments. Even its **gramadevatas** were particularised.

The land under cultivation was assigned to individual families of cultivators who had a hereditary right to cultivate, provided the share of the landowner was regularly paid, but the cultivator was not considered the proprietor. The waste-lands and the grazing pastures were the common property of the village or of the King. The King might assign usufructuary rights on portions of this lot to Brahamans as **Agrahara** or to others for performance of services, but these rights were subject to resumption.

Village isolation, primitive techniques of production and administrative autonomy were strong inducements for resisting the encroachments and intervention of external agencies. They conflicted with the centripetal forces of political organisation. But only because the villages were poorly equipped for armed resistance they had to yield to the force at the command of kings and chiefs. When they compensated for what they received from the villages in taxes by supplying the needs for irrigation, communication and security, the payment was willing, otherwise when their levies were collected merely by superior force, the payment was unwilling. The development of this type of village economy gave strong support to the evolution of what may be called the feudal polity. Fiefs began to be granted to high officers.

Information about the industry of the north during this period is scanty, nor is our knowledge of internal and external trade very satisfactory. All that can be said is that the Kushana, Saka and Pahlava domination in the northern and the western parts and the existence of the Parthian empire in the west must have kept the trade routes open. Their rule was responsible for the penetration of Buddhism into Central Asia and China. Indian monk scholars travelled to China and translated Buddhist texts into the Chinese and other languages. It was in this manner that Asvaghosh's **Buddha Charita** reached Khotan and was adapted into the Khotanese, Sogdian and numerous other languages. At last it reached Iran, Mesopotamia and Armenia under the title of Budasaf wa Baluhar. Mani who was the prophet of the syncretist faith called himself the Buddha.

From the periplus of the Erytherian Sea we learn that there were trade routes connecting the capital of the Scythian Satraps, Minnager with Kabul, and Baroach with Central Asia. Isidore of Charax gives the itinerary of a merchant from Antioch to the river Helmand on the border of Afghanistan.

But the evidence of trade with the South is ampler, and shows that the exchanges between India and western and eastern lands were abundant. The southern trade was very largely seaborne. The commodities exported were mostly products of the South—ivory, pearls, textiles—fine and coarse, precious stones, and aromatics. The imports consisted of metals, gold especially, wines, slave girls, etc. In order to handle the large commerce many ports were developed on the coast line and market towns grew up on the routes into the interior.

Trade with eastern countries and with China was also brisk. Overland the route proceeded from Taxila to Kabul, Bamian, over the Hindukush, Bactria, and thence joined the silk route to China either by way of Khotan and Yarkand or across the Taklamakan desert to Kucha and Karashar.

Again the sea route was more frequented. Indians had established regular traffic from the ports of the Coromandal Coast to Malaya and Cambodia in the second and third centuries A.D. and they had founded Indian principalities in these eastern regions. The trade with China also grew up and large Chinese ships came to the southern ports of India and exchanged goods which were carried in Arab bottoms to the west.

The stimulus that trade gave to the social and political life of the South was great, as appears from the history of the Pallavas, Pandyas, Cheras and Cholas in the South and the Chalukyas and Rashtrakutas in the Deccan.

It was during this period that the stratification of the social system acquired its rigidity. Although the general structure of society was based on the differentiation of **Varna** (class) and **Jati** (caste), the different regions of India developed different combinations of these social divisions. The first noticeable characteristic is that caste instead of being tribal has become predominantly regional. Each region has its own caste system and as some puranas point out there were only two castes left after Mahapadma Nanda, namely, the Brahmanas and Sudras, which is nearly true of the South and the East. The Brahamans are divided into ten sections—five Gauda and five Dravida, and their sub-castes, too, are largely regional. They hardly have any occupational subsections.

The Kshatriyas were originally Rajanya chiefs, nobles and military officers. Then some tribal groups or **ganas** acquired the designation, e.g., Yaudheyas, Malavas, Arjunayanas. Kautilya speaks of Kamboja and Surastra corporations of Kshtriyas practising **Varta** (husbandry and trade) along with military professions while tribes like the Lichhavis, Vrijikas, Mallas, Gurus and Panchalas were only warriors and rulers. The Kshatriyas, too, had become a caste, who were later divided into Surya and Chandra Vamsis and Agni Kulas. They, too, could not be divided into oçcupational subcastes. The two castes–the Brahmanas and Kshatriyas, formed the upper stratum of society, although within each of them there were higher and lower categories. Together they must have formed a small proportion of the population of a region.

The Vaisyas and the Sudras constituted with the outcastes the main body of society in each territory. Their sections were based largely on occupation although race and locality also played a part. The Vaisyas who were originally the third group of the Aryan tribes, had fallen on evil days and were assimilated with the Sudras, although theoretically they were still reckoned among the Dwijas. There were again two classes among the Vaisyas–the well-to-do and influential groups of Sethis, Grihapatis and Kutumbikas and the others working as agriculturists, traders and craftsmen.

On the other hand, the Sudra status had improved partly as a result of the transfer of very mean employments to the untouchables, of the increase in the value of the products of crafts, and the admission of many foreigners in society.

But the worst feature of this hardening of the caste system was the introduction of the principle of differential rights. Not only were marriage, social status, and profession determined on the basis of caste, almost every social activity was actually or supposedly regulated by it. For instance, the forms of address were different–**ehi, agachha, adrava, adhava,**[1] the size of funeral cakes (**pindas**), the performance of religious rites, the chanting of the mantras, the punishment for crimes, the rates of interest, the opportunities for education, all differed from one caste to another. The inevitable result of the system was that

1 Satapatha Brahmana i. 1, 4, 12. Dutt, N.K., *The Origin and Growth of caste in India,* p. 85.

all sense of identification of the interests of the part with those of the whole was lost, and therefore when invaders came the few Kshatriyas with their retainers resisted and fought, but the main body of the people looked on unconcerned. Hence in spite of the overwhelming numbers of the Hindus and the valour and heroism of the warriors, the handicaps were so great as to ensure almost certain defeat.

The **Smritis** which were the product of this period uphold fully these differences. The Brahmans are raised to the very highest status and endowed with all kinds of privileges. There is, however, some doubt whether in actual practice they were so treated. The Buddhist works of the period assign to them a position lower than that of the Kshatriyas. It is also noticeable that all of them did not follow the duties prescribed for them and the **Smritis** had to make allowances for them and permit them to follow non-Brahmanic occupations. On the other hand, there are facts which indicate the pre-eminence of the Brahmans. For instance, the dynasty of the Sungas who followed the Mauryas was Brahman, so were their successors the Kanvas. The Satavahanas took pride in calling themselves Brahmans. Again the large output of literature in Sanskrit and the nearly complete monopoly of knowledge in all its branches indicate unchallenged intellectual ascendancy of the Brahmans.

By the time the Gupta empire came to be established in the fourth century A.D. the social evolution of India had been completed. The rigid caste system, the self-sufficient village economy, and the hierarchic feudal polity had been firmly established. Their hold was so strong that the Muslim conquest and dominion which began in the eleventh and lasted till the middle of the eighteenth century A.D. was unable to mitigate its rigours. Nearly two hundred years of British rule made radical changes in this economic and social order but the system has not yet completely disintegrated.

The Guptas and the Vardhanas raised their political structures on these foundations. Their success deepened and broadened them, so the Hindu society became static, unalterable and impregnable. The greatness of the Gupta empire, however, was due to adventitious circumstances, which is proved by the fact that no sooner had they passed away than India fell back into internal anarchy and political disarray.

The third century A.D. saw the decline of the Kushanas who were brought under the empire of the Iranian Sasanids. The Pahlava and Saka satraps of western India were extinguished by the Guptas. The result was that intercourse between India and its western neighbours became free, and not only did Indian goods find a growing market in Central Asia, the Iranian empire, the Fertile Crescent, and the Mediterranean world, Indian cultural influences spread all over the world. A great resurgence of arts and industry and renaissance of intellect swept the country. It was an age of wealth, luxury and refinement. It saw the development of the wonderful rock hewn cave architecture, with sculpture and painting decoration of the Chaitya halls and Viharas of Karli, Ajanta, and Ellora, and the temples of Devagarh and Gaya. Their richness, variety and skill is unparalleled in the history of the world art. The exceeding abundance of statuary and mural paintings is proof of the immeasurable fulness and outpouring of life. Apparently joy and hope filled the hearts of men and found expression in the lithic lyricism and colour rhythms of art.

There was little that was other worldly or ascetical or life-negating in the ensemble of figures and the scenes depicted on the ceilings and walls of the temples and monasteries. In fact, it is amazing that these halls of religious worship and cloisters for the residence of monks were adorned with pictures of all the phases of worldly life—love and passion; fun and frolic; feasts and drinking parties; royal coronation durbars and processions; the march of armies and the din and bustle of the market place. The men portrayed are ordinarily young, robust and energetic; women beautiful, slender, with bare bosoms, dreamy eyes and attractive coiffures.

What is true of art is equally applicable to literature which rose to heights never reached before or after in Sanskrit language. In poetry and drama the greatest name is that of Kalidasa, but among others not far behind were Bhavabhuti and Sri Harsha; in Kavya Bharavi and Magha; in lyric poetry Bhartrihari; in fables Somadeva, author of **Kathasaritasagara**, Kshemendra, the author of **Brhat-Kathamanjari** and **Gunadhya**; in romance Dandin and Bana. Their main themes were love, adventure, valour, **jois de vivre**; for which the witnesses are Kalidasa's **Rtusamhara, Meghaduta, Kumara Sambhava,** and **Raghuvansa.**

Nor were the sciences neglected. Grammar, meteorology, politics, law, medicine, astronomy and mathematics were all cultivated, as also philosophy and religion. It is symptomatic of the times that the science of love, **Kamasutra**, was treated as a special science.

With the picture of the youngman about town in the **Kamasutra**, the Beau Brummel of the Gupta age, I will bring this discourse to an end. Listen to the description of Vatasyayana:

The Nagaraka is a wealthy citizen enjoying the fellowship of boon companions and ladies of the demi monde. His house is filled with luxuries of the age—canopies, pillows, mirrors, perfumes, musical instruments; his garden is strewn with flowers, and swings hang from the branches of the trees for the amusement of his lady friends. He rises in the morning, takes his bath, anoints his body with unguents and perfumes, puts collyrium on his eyes, red lac on his lips, and chews a betel. He takes his meals, teaches the parrots and mynahs, watches fighting cocks, quails or rams, and takes a nap in the afternoon. He attends with his friends—Vitas, Pithamardas, Vidusakas, music parties, dance shows and theatrical performances. He has intellectual interests, too. He knows the sixty-four arts, makes poems, and recites them in poetical gatherings. He may also be a painter. But he is no vulgar sensualist. Even the hetairae, with whom he dallies and who constitute an essential part of his life, are accomplished ladies adorned with learning, poetry and music so that he greatly enjoys their company and their conversation which is both refined and intellectually satisfying.

Evidently ancient Indian society was not all spiritual mysticism, self-denial and renunciation.

2

INDIA IN THE MIDDLE AGES

The history of the Middle Ages is not as tantalising in facts and dates as that of the ancient times. For one thing much more material for the centuries following the death of Harsha is available concerning both political and cultural history than for the earlier age. Secondly, its chronology is more certain, and the accounts left by the foreigners, specially the Arab travellers and geographers, more plentiful.

After the tenth century the Persian chronicles become available and they throw much light upon the deeds of the new actors who appear upon the Indian stage.

These Persian chronicles, as Dodwell admits, are far superior to the English medieval chronicles, so that "the Muslim period is one of vivid living men whereas the Hindu period is one of shadows."[1] But they possess many virtues as well as defects. Both of these are in the main the result of the peculiar origin and development of history-writing under Islamic civilisation. Historical enquiry came to birth among the Arabs as a

1 Dodwell–*India*, 1, 22-23 (Hardy, 115).

handmaid of theology. The problems that worried theologians in the early times were connected with the compilation and interpretation of the **Quran** and the **Hadith.** For the proper understanding of the significance of an **Ayat** (verse) it was necessary to know the occasion, the time and place of its communication. In the case of the Prophet's sayings and actions such knowledge was indeed indispensable. Determination of these facts was the business of the historian. Later when interested people began to collect the sayings of the Prophet (**Hadith**), it was essential to distinguish between what was genuine and what was spurious, and therefore to adopt strict methods of testing the reliability of persons who handed them down. The next stage was to prepare the biographies (**Sirat**) of the Prophet, and of his wars and campaigns (**maghazi**). Later still the Arab conquests and annexations raised problems concerning the character of the occupation, and the status of the annexed lands. This was necessary because the rates and manner of the payment of revenue depended upon it.

Such practical needs obliged scholars to undertake historical studies. Soon other needs appeared. The rulers were confronted with administrative problems, for whose solution they naturally turned to precedents in the past. For example, Caliph Mansur the Abbasid wanted to get rid of his dangerously able and popular Vizier Abu Muslim Khurasani and turned to historians to help him out of the situation. They told him the story of Shapur the Sasanian Emperor of Iran, who had in somewhat similar circumstances sent his Vizier to Khorasan to bring the rebellious people there to order. His success made Shapur jealous and afraid. So he recalled the Vizier, cut off his head and threw it before the Khorasanis, who were duly impressed and frightened into submission.

Thus historiography became popular for edificatory and practical purposes. **Kashf al Zunun** enumerates 1,300 histories which were known to its author, and they were only a part of the several thousand which had been compiled.

The historians who wrote the chronicles in India had, in this way, numerous examples to follow, and naturally in doing so they imbibed both the merits and shortcomings of their masters. Jurji Zaydan points out their defects as follows:

(1) The historians were satisfied with nothing the source and authority for their statements, but did not discuss their reason and logic and made no scientific enquiry.

(2) The contents of such histories were limited to wars and victories, appointment and dismissal of officials, and births and deaths, but there was no reflection on science and literature, on social conditions, on evolution of culture, and on causes and effects of political circumstances.

(3) The histories were uncritical. They were written with the desire to win the approval of their co-religionists and therefore they refrained from criticising the Musalmans on the ground of faith and theology. They also sought to gain favours from man in power. Sabi a historian of Al Buyah confessed, "I weave together a lot of lies, fiddle faddle and silly nonsense":

"یک مشت دروغ و چند و پرنگی بافم۔"

(4) **Odium theologicum** provided strong motivation. It sometimes led to vulgarity and abuse.

A vast majority of the Muslim chroniclers belonged to the class of the Ulama, who may be divided into three categories. Those who happened to belong to some Sufi order, like the Chishtia, and remained independent and refused to dance attendance upon the rulers. The other two were: (1) flatterers who received court patronage, and (2) calumniators that is those who were rebuffed in favour of their rivals. It is difficult to find among such writers scientific detachment like that of an Al Biruni or Ibn i Khaldun.

The Muslim Ulama's concept of history was basically theological. They looked upon human history as "the march of Providence upon earth," and they believed that Providence manifested itself in Islam, which was the eternal religion, which existed from the beginning of the world and would continue to exist to the end till its destiny was fulfilled. There is an **Ayat** in the **Quran (Surah Yunus)** which puts these words in the mouth of Moses and indicates that Moses was a believer in Islam:

وَقَالَ مُوسَىٰ يٰقَوْمِ اِنْ كُنْتُمْ بِاللهِ   فَعَلَيْهِ تَوَكَّلُوْا اِنْ كُنْتُمْ مُسْلِمِيْنَ ۔

"Musa said, O my people, if you believe in God, in Him put your trust, if you are Muslims (have surrendered)." –**Surah Yunus** 84.

Hence the history of the Muslim community **(Ummat)** which was actualised through the Prophet Muhammad is the divine epiphany, would fulfil itself in the perfection of the community of the faithful.

It is some such notion of history which the Muslim chroniclers sought to express in their writings. Zia ud Din Barani, for instance, enumerated seven excellences which appertain to history. Among them the two first are, (1) history is the same as the knowledge contained in the holy scriptures, and (2) it is identical with **Hadith,**

(وعلم التاريخ توامان علم الحديث)

He praises history because of its moralising role. It stabilises the mind, teaches patience and submission, promotes virtue and trains reason, understanding and judgment. For him history occupied the fifth position after the science of Quranic exigesis, tradition, jurisprudence and mysticism. Although its importance was recognised, history was not prescribed as a subject in the curricula of the schools.

Barani's ideal historian was a scholar who was morally truthful and religiously sound. But he was an aristocrat. It was his duty to collect together traditions and news about great prophets, caliphs, monarchs, religious leaders and great men," but to refrain from collecting information about "the low, mean, unworthy, crushed, base, small minded, ignoble, miserly, rascally, humble, ignoble and huckstering." History therefore should deal with the elite and not with the common people. It was concerned with the deeds of great men and not with mass movements and social evolution. As the great were the gift of God, not the natural order but the divine order was the proper subject of history, and it was futile to seek in it rational concatenation of events.

The Ulama although self-constituted custodians of Islam departed violently from some of the fundamental principles of the faith. The fact that they belonged to the ruling class made them repudiate the basic Islamic tenet of the equality of all men. They only cared for the higher classes (the **Ashraf** and the **Aiyan**) and completely ignored the humble and the low (the **Ajlaf**), both Hindu and Muslim. They were supposed to be the propagators of Islam, but in fact this task was left largely to the mystics and the missionaries. The Ulama depended for their livelihood upon the patronage of the state or of the people. They were employed in the capacity of **Qazi, Mufti, Muhtasib, Imam** and teacher. They were like the Brahmans, holding the monopoly of learning which conferred upon them the status of a highly privileged class. Their claims were high; "the Ulama are the heirs of the Prophet." According to them, the Prophet had said, "the best kings and the best nobles are those who visit the doors of the Ulama and the nobles."

It is a sad fact that a great many of them waited at the doors of the kings and nobles. They were **Ulamai Duniya** (worldly minded), or **Ulamai-Su** (evil). Unfortunately the epithet was freely bandied about between the jealous aspirants for favours, and history is full of the din of controversy and intrigue in which the Ulama indulged. But a rather sinister aspect of the situation was that they sought to interfere actively in politics and to influence the policies of government. Throughout the Middle Ages this factor was much in evidence in the activities of the state. The Ulama endeavoured to guide the state in accordance with what they considered were the injunctions of religion, on the contrary the rulers sought to steer the ship of the state according to the assessment of what the situation demanded.

As medieval historiography was largely in the hands of the Ulama the religious bias greatly influenced their writings. They have infected even the modern historians. British writers like Elliot and James Mill used the chronicles written by the Ulama to justify British rule and to show the intolerance and hostility of the Muslim rulers towards their subjects in order to bring into relief their own superiority. The Indian writers under their influence have projected the contemporary communal antagonisms on to the medieval scene. They read in these far off events a reflection of the sentiments which motivate the present generation.

With the peculiar slant of the source books of Indian history emanating from the theological composers and the strong prejudices which pervade the minds of modern writers, difficulties of interpreting the events of the medieval times become enormously multiplied. But it is necessary both for the sake of academic rectitude and of civic duty to make the attempt to analyse the record dispassionately.

At the very start of our enquiry we are faced with the problem which is undoubtedly unpleasant, namely, how to account for the defeat and failure of the Indian principalities at the hands of foreign aggressors, first in the eighth and then in the eleventh century and after.

The conquest of Sindh in 712 A.D. by Muhammad bin Qasim a young lad of just over sixteen years of age is an amazing military feat, specially if it is remembered that the Arab forces had to march hundreds of miles through the most inhospitable territory of Makran and Baluchistan—a rainless desert cut up by dry beds of streams, shifting sanddunes and bare hillocks. Yet in spite of the length of communications and hard logistic perplexities Sindh and Multan were overrun. Similarly Mahmud of Ghazni and the Shansabani Sultans of Ghor wreaked their will on the capitals of states and holy places of India scattered over wide distances from Banaras to

Somanath. These exploits are extraordinary and need explaining. Some of the explanations given by Indian historians seem fantastic, especially those which lay undue emphasis upon the factor of religion.

Our historians do not sufficiently clearly realise that all wars are basically promoted by political and economic interests. But because they involve much cruelty, violence, destruction of life and property, they exert a fearful strain upon the more humane feelings of man. In order to overcome the inner moral conflict or to escape its confrontation man resorts to rationalisations and justifications. Religion, national honour, ethical principles, are appealed to in order to cover the hideously gory realities as greed for wealth and lust for power. The ostensible and avowed aim of war becomes a camouflage for its real purpose. Hindus, Muslims and Christians though differing in their religion have all behaved alike in this matter.

This is what Pierre Bayle (1647-1706) in his **Dictionnaire historique et critique** (1697) wrote concerning the role of religion in human affairs:

"The kings of France resorted to Mahometan methods for establishing Christianity in Frisia and in Saxony, and the same violent means were used to establish it in Scandinavia.... The same methods were resorted to for dealing with (Christian) sects that dared to condemn the Pope; and they are going to be resorted to in India as soon as the power to apply them is there."

According to Bayle the Muhammedans were obliged by religious principle to use violence (which is not true), "yet, in spite of that, they have been tolerating other religions for some centuries past. The Christians have not been given orders to do anything but preach and instruct; yet, in spite of this, from time immemorial they have been exterminating by fire and sword all those who are not of their religion."[1]

1 Toynbee: A historians approach to Religion pp. 205-6.

The Crusades (from the end of the eleventh to the end of the thirteenth century) were no less inspired by the lure of eastern trade than the desire to recover the holy lands. The so-called Wars of Religion which led to horrible massacres in France and vast devastation in Central Europe in the sixteenth and seventeenth centuries were an expression of the conflict of the national interests of classes and the ambitions of military chiefs and kings like Gustavas Vasa. Religion was a cloak to conceal the truth.

The conquests of Muhammad bin Qasim, the raids of Mahmud of Ghazni and the Turkish invasions were no different, for in spite of what the Muslim medieval chroniclers say in their justification or the contemporary self-styled objective historians assert, it will be a travesty of historical verity to regard them otherwise. The considerations which prompted the invasions and the causes of their success must be sought so much in religious fanaticism and the determination to propagate religion as in the ambition for territorial aggrandisement, and the exploitation of opportunities held out by the weaknesses of the victims.

It is necessary to analyse the internal conditions which invited aggression and the intentions and actions of the aggressors in order to understand the why and wherefore of these astoundingly stirring occurrences.

What then does history tell us of India on the eve of the Arab invasion of Sindh? The first thing that it says is that in the eighth century no entity existed which socially, politically, or even geographically corresponded to the name India. Before the foreigners had given the name **Hind** to our country there was no term in Sanskrit to designate it. Jambudvipa denoted one of the seven continents containing India, Aryavarta the land between the eastern and western seas and the Himalaya and Vindhya mountains, and Brahmavarta, the tract between the Saraswati and Drishadvati. Bharatavarsha first occurs in the **Kavya Sisupalabaddha** of Magha who has been assigned to the eighth or ninth century, and it is doubtful whether it applied to non-Aryan India.

Nor did there exist any social entity known as **Hindu.** The peoples of India, whatever their religion, did not constitute a single community, a social unity or individuality. There was no coherence among the inhabitants of India, no organisation binding the parts into a whole. They were not like the Christians of medieval Europe from the Atlantic to Russia, who for religious purposes were under the authority of the Pope of Rome; nor even like the Muslims of the eighth and ninth centuries who owed allegiance to the Caliph at Baghdad.

There existed in India a plurality of societies independent of one another. They shared a common culture, especially religious, like the independent Christian societies of Europe. Each had its own educated class which consisted of the Brahmans whose language of learning was Sanskrit. But the spoken language of the people differed from region to region. In some regions, for instance, in the Tamilnad the spoken language had evolved into a rich literary language, and similar developments were on the way in others—Maharashtri and the Prakrits.

The caste divisions within each society were so sharp that it is doubtful whether any society could be regarded as a community. The rights and privileges of the higher castes, which were hereditary and therefore unattainable by the other castes, distinguished them from the vast numbers of the lower castes. The prohibitions regarding connubium (right of marriage) and commensality (right of eating together) were so strict—Varahamihr adds to them by assigning different quarters of a city to the four castes, fixing different number of dwellings for each of them and prescribing different regulations for the use of chowries and umbrellas, as to make any real sympathy or strong fellow feeling between different sections of society almost impossible. It was only the monopoly of arms and political power and of knowledge and education of the upper strata which held them together in those economically static conditions.

It may, however, be admitted that caste although a tremendous handicap in confrontations with foreigners like the Arabs and the Turks, was no serious disadvantage, when Indian communities similarly organised came into conflict and waged wars. Moreover, caste secured by its differentiation of functions unique opportunities for the class reserved for study and teaching to specialise in the promotion of knowledge. The Brahman released from all other encumbrances and worldly cares devoted himself to literary pursuits. It must be acknowledged that he made a very good use of his opportunities. The literature which he produced is unparalleled in its depth, extent and force. In its vast sweep it comprehends all or almost all aspects and deliverances of human mind—religion, philosophy, mathematics, science, literature—prose, poetry, drama, stories and the arts. And what a magnificent pile altogether do they make!

Politically the diversity was even more marked. Technical backwardness—lack of means of rapid movement and communication, primitive arms and weapons, comparative ease of defence in walled villages and cities and moat-protected rampart-enclosed fortresses made rebellion against authority easy and maintenance of control over unruly elements difficult. Society was a compound of feudal landlords, chiefs and princes. Government was largely indirect through feudal hierarchies, except in the narrow region round the centre of power. According to Kautilya's theory every **mandala** or circle of authority was surrounded by a belt of powers necessarily hostile and this was in turn surrounded by a belt of possible allies.

Thus every Indian principality was immediately surrounded by neighbours who were its enemies and mediately by states which were enemies of these immediate neighbours. A posture of things which admitted of no universal political order.

From time to time, out of the multiplicity of autonomous principalities larger political organisations were built up, sometimes deserving the title of empire, as happened in the third century B.C. and fourth century A.D. and to a lesser extent under Harsha in the north and the Satavahanas and the Cholas in the South. But the normal condition was that of mutually hostile plurality of principalitics endeavouring to destroy one another.

The list of the nine divisions of India given by Varahamihira together with the names of tribes and people residing in them is a witness to the divisions which prevailed in that age—seventh century A.D. It is confirmed by all modern histories. India in the eighth century was a patchwork of numerous states, each made up of many parts held together in uneasy partnership and obedience by an overlord. War was almost perennial between neighbours and none seems to have entertained any scruples in using Machiavellian strategems against another, or against pretenders and rivals constantly threatening disruption and revolt from within.

It must also be conceded that the state of morals was at its nadir in these times. Literature furnishes ample evidence of this melancholy state of affairs. Damodara Gupta, poet and minister of Jayapida of Kashmir (779-813 A.D.), wrote an erotic comic work **Kuttanimatam**, which throws a lurid light upon the manners of the men of the upper class—sensual fools and unmitigated rogues. It is a squalid tale in which prostitutes, precuresses, young philanderers and cheats abound.

Damodara Gupta was followed by Kshemendra of the eleventh century, another Kashmirian poet well known for his **Brhat Kathamanjari.** His **Samaya Matrika** (mother by convention) is the story of a young courtesan, a roguish barber and an "owl faced, crow necked and cat eyed" old bawd—all constituting a world of cheats, knaves, dolts, and of repulsive profligacy and sordid behaviour. Similar in spirit is the Narmamala which is a bitter satire on the misconduct and abuse of power on the part of the myrmidons of government.

Krishna Misra a contemporary of Kshemendra living in the domain of the Chandellas draws a picture of the moral struggle within the soul of man and incidentally describes the prevalence of unethical doctrines and superstitious cults in those times.

But the most telling account of the wickedness, corruption and intrigue of the princes and noblemen is vividly set out in Kalhana's **Rajatarigni** completed in 1149-50. The narrative containing the story of Kashmir in the times of the author (1112-50) is one of unmitigated misrule, of luxury loving voluptuaries, absolute tyrants who oppressed and plundered the people, cruelly persecuted their feudal barons, and promoted rebellion, murder and rapine. For example, Harsha (1089-1101), with whom the new dynasty of Lohara began its rule, is described by Stein as a king of "Nero-like propensities". His end was violent. His successor Ucchala was engaged in patricidal wars. His two successors were puppets whose rule lasted together for four months. The reign of the next ruler Sussala was one long disaster—fire, famine, rebellion, civil war and murder.

Jayasimha occupied the throne after his father for a long time (1128-55), but internal strife and disruptive tendencies bedevilled his reign. Treason and rebellion stalked and harried the land.

The political conditions of Kalhan's times had a great deal to do with the formation of the character of the people. He is painfully aware of "the conspicuous want of physical and moral courage" in them, "of the inveterate cowardice and empty bragging of the Kashmirian soldiery"; and he bitterly deplores the readiness of those in positions of influence to desert or sell their masters, or the callous indifference with which Kashmirian populace was prepared to welcome any change.

Alberuni who was an extremely fair and objective student of Hindu religion and philosophy and a sympathetic critic of Hindu manners and character writes in his **Kitab al-Hind,** compiled more than a hundred years before **Rajatarangini,** as follows:

"at the utmost, they fight with words, but they will never

stake their soul or body or their property on religious controversy."[1]

It is true that they possessed some fine qualities such as tolerance, good faith, fidelity, justice, as attested by the Arab writers like Idrisi and the Venetian Marco Polo who visited the south of India in 1292. But the testimony regarding the character of the higher classes is overwhelmingly unfavourable to them. This is borne out by the history of the conquest of Sindh by Muhammad bin Quasim.

Even before him the Arabs had been skirmishing round both on sea and land probing the strength and weakness of the rulers of Sindh, but when they made with full preparation their final assault, the kingdom fell apart like a house of cards.

According to the accounts of Huien Tsiang (seventh centuary A.D.) Sindh was an extensive and powerful kingdom. **Chach Namah** indicates that it extended in the west to Makran, in the north to Kashmir, in the east to the Kingdom of Kanauj, and in the south to the sea. Obviously its subjects were not homogeneous either from the religious or the social point of view. There were many tribes and small principalities which were kept together by force. Their loyalty to the state was undependable for neither community of religion, nor of race, nor of homeland could overcome their love for tribal or local autonomy. Not only were their chieftains perpetually at war against the central government, inside the government itself there was continuous tussle for power. In the pursuit of their particularist selfish interests they appeared to make no distinction between foreigner and native, alien and non-alien.

Chach the Brahman chamberlain of Sahasi Rai the ruler of Sindh who succeeded him on the throne, founded a new dynasty. There was apparently no unity between the Brahman usurper and the Buddhists of Sindh, or between him and the Jat tribes. According to Sisakar, the Hindu minister of Dahir

1 Sachan, F. S. Alberuni's India. vol. I, p. 19.

who deserted to Muhammad bin Qasim, Chach had imposed most humiliating conditions on the Jats. They were not allowed to wear fine clothes, cover their heads or put on shoes, or ride on saddled horses. They had to perform enforced duties as escorts, as suppliers or firewood for the royal kitchen and as menials and guards. If any member of the tribe committed a theft, they had to punish him by burning him and his family and children. Naturally the Jats favoured the enemy of their oppressors.

Was then the invasion inspired by religion, and were the defenders fighting for their faith? Facts do not entirely support the theory. For instance, a number of prominent and influential Hindus favoured Qasim. Among them were Sisakar the minister of Dahir, Moka Bisaya the chief of a tribe, Ladi Dahir's Queen who married Qasim after her husband's death and actually induced the besieged Hindus of Bahmanabad to surrender. On the other side, Allafi an Arab commander of Arab horsemen fought on the side of Dahir and was his adviser. No Hindu ruler raised his little finger in support of Dahir, nor did his son who appealed for help to his brother and nephews do so to other Hindu chiefs.

These men did not lose their dominion because they were cowardly. In fact Dahir and his son Jaisiya are described by the Muslim chronicler as "unequalled in bravery and wisdom". They were vanquished partly because of the superior fighting equipment of their conquerors, but mainly because Hindu social and political systems placed them at a great disadvantage against their enemies. It must be remembered that the Arabs possessed better horses with greater manoeuvrability, that possibly their bows and arrows were more effective, their lances lighter, and swords sharper. They were more united because they were less burdened by social inequalities and divisions.

It is a remarkable fact that the Hindus easily won the confidence of the Muslims and vice versa. Hindu chiefs surrendered in many cases without resistance merely on the assurance of humane treatment, Hindu defenders deserted by their leaders submitted and were not molested. The only exceptions were men bearing arms who were not spread. Muhammad bin Qasim took Shiskar into his confidence and told him all his secrets, he relied upon Moka Bisaya to lead foraging parties against Jaisiya, and appointed Kaksa cousin of Dahir as his Vizier with precedence over all Muslim nobles and army commanders. These facts lend no colour to the widely held belief of historians that the invasion of Sindh was a religious crusade. The results do not justify this conclusion either. It is doubtful whether many Sindhis were converted to Islam by the invaders, for till long after there were large number of Hindus in the province. Their places of worship were not damaged as is proved by the case of the temple at Multan;[1] many Brahmans were employed in the administration. The Sumras who ruled over Sindh bore Hindu names, but whether they were Ismailis or Hindus is difficult to decide. Their successors were the Sammas whose religious convictions are equally uncertain. They seem to be the same Jat clan which was oppressed by Chach. As late as 1699 Captain A. Hamilton found the number of Hindus ten times that of the Muslims in Thatta. The Hindu **Amils** were the official class under the Kalhoras and Talpurs.

The history of Sindh shows that the factor of religion has been exaggerated. In this connection an item of information given both by **Chach Namah** and **Futuh al Buldan** of Al Biladhuri is most interesting. They state that Hajjaj the Governor of Iraq who had despatched Muhammad bin Qasim on the campaign had a balance sheet of the war prepared, which showed that 60,000 silver **dirhems** was the expenditure and 120,000 **dirhems** the income from the campaign. Biladhuri has changed thousands into millions. Apparently the expedition was as much a business enterprise as a venture for the expansion of the empire. But while the principals in the enterprise were reckoning their gains in territory and revenue, the scho-

1 Idrisi in the 11th and Quazvini in the 13th century mention the existence of the temple. The French traveller Thavenot describes it in A.D. 1666.

lars were gloating over the successes in terms of conversions and killings of the infidels and demolition of their places of worship, in disregard of what the realities were.

I have narrated the story of Sindh in some detail in order to explain the causes and consequences of the first Muslim invasion of India. For the next three centuries India had a respite from foreign invasions. The way opened by Muhammad bin Qasim presented far too many difficulties to be of much use for exploitation, and then the decline of the power of the Abbasid Caliphate reduced the force which had supplied the initial impetus. Therefore the Arab governors in Sindh—at Mansura and Multan, lost the capability to extend Muslim rule from these centres. It was not so much the increase in the power of Indian resistance as the loss of initiative and drive, because of the absence of support from Baghdad, that accounts for the temporary halt of conquest.

The Abbasids had lost Spain, Morocco, Tunis, Egypt that is, the whole of North Africa by 870 A.D., Yaman in Arabia, Syria and Mesopotamia about 60 years after, eastern Persia in the beginning of the ninth century A.D. and northern Persia along the southern coast of the Caspian by the middle of the ninth century. In the tenth century A.D. the Buwaihids has established their control over western Persia and Iraq including Baghdad; and the Samanids had taken hold of the north-western region on the borders of India. These losses were mainly responsible for the inability of the Arab rulers of Sindh to exert their efforts with any strength in the direction of the east, although raids and skirmishes continued.

By the tenth century A.D. the unity of Islamic countries under the central authority of the Caliph of Baghdad lay shattered. The ambitious local chiefs, the Sultans, had declared their independence and henceforth their internecine quarrels, intrigues for expansion of dominion and rivalries fill the pages of history. With these developments the zeal for religion was replaced by that for material gain, of which the conquest of Sindh is one illustration.

Another is furnished by the Indian raids of Mahmud of Ghazni. Even a cursory perusal of the activities of Mahmud shows that his aims were not the propagation of the faith or the exaltation of the glory of Islam, but purely territorial aggrandisement and plunder. It is true that he was honoured with the high sounding titles like the **'Ramin al Daulah wa Amir al Millat'**, by Caliph al Qadir, but this was a reward for Mahmud's support of Qadir against the Samanid Amir Nuh bin Mansur who refused to recognise him. In later life Mahmud himself intended to bring the Caliph under his control.

Mahmud was undoubtedly the greatest general of his age, and perhaps one of the greatest of all times, who by his matchless skill and indefatigable energy overturned numerous principalities, vanquished a host of chiefs, devastated cities, sacked and pillaged temples and harried vast regions from Ispahan in the west to Banaras in the east. But in spite of the eulogies of his blind admirers like the historian Utbi, the poets Farrukhi and Unsuri and their modern imitators, he remains in the category of such world shakers as Atilla and Chingiz who rendered little service to religion or human progress. Firdausi called him a King who knew neither faith nor law nor manners.

That Mahmud possessed no evangelical zeal is evident. With rare exceptions he made no conversions. His razzias in India had only one object—to collect gold, silver, precious stones, elephants and slaves. It is calculated that he took away more than one hundred and fifty crore of rupees worth of gold and silver besides large quantities of jewels, several hundred elephants and numerous slaves who were sold cheap in the markets of central Asia.

All over the north-western region—Central Asia, Khurasan, Sistan, Baluchistan, Islam was the dominant religion, but there were numerous non-Muslims—Hindus and Buddhists, scattered about in these lands. Many of them served in Mahmud's armies fighting under his banner in India, Central Asia and Iran. In Ghazni the capital there was a separate quarter reserved for them where they lived freely practising the rites of their faith. His elephant drivers were Hindus and several Hindu names occur among his officers, e.g., Tilak, Sunder, Sivand Rai.

Nor was the truth about Mahmud's intentions, beliefs and morals wholly unknown to his contemporaries. He fought wars and rained horrors—looting, burning, killing, upon Hindus and Muslims alike. The Carmathians were perhaps the worst sufferers among his victims. It is difficult to say which of the religious injunctions—commands and prohibitions, he actually carried out. He loved war, wine and women and was fond of poetry and music. Yet his career was held as a warning for the instability of wealth and the futility of power rather than as an example of righteousness.

The story of Qazi Abul Hasan and his son as told by Baihaqi shows that there were in those days pious Ulama who refused to touch the gold, which in their poverty they desperately needed because of the unlawful manner of its acquisition.

If the religious motive in Mahmud's achievements wears rather thin, its relevance to the behaviour of his Hindu opponents is even less convincing. In northern India which bore the brunt of Mahmud's violence there were from Assam to Kabul, numerous Hindu states, petty and large. There was no understanding, co-operation, much less alliance or federation, or awareness of religious unity among them.

The smaller ones were as bellicose against their neighbours, as the larger ones, but it is neither possible nor profitable to try and extricate their mutual relations and the kaleidoscopic changes in them. Even the greater chiefs found their hold on their territories menaced by their own fellow believers continuously from within and without. One or two instances of their troublesome predicament may be supplied. When Mahmud was storming the northern Indian cities, Mahipala was building his empire in Eastern India. Not only was he annexing territories in West, East, North and South Bengal, but also in north Bihar. He had, besides, to repel the invasions of

Rajendra Chola from the South and of the Kalachuris of Madhya Pradesh.

In Kanauj the Pratiharas ruled. But their power had been weakened by the attacks of the Rashtrakutas. Krishna II, Indra III, and Krishna III who advanced to the gates of the city between A.D. 915 and 918 and again in A.D. 940 and 963, after which there was a steady decline in their power. The rise of the Chandellas, Kalachuris and Chalukyas, gave further blows to their declining authority. It is therefore unwarranted to hold that they acted as a bulwark against the aggression of the Turkish hordes.

The Chandellas were the enemies of the Pratiharas. They called themselves "a scorching fire to the Gurjaras". Their king Yasovarman seized Kalinjar and occupied the territory of Kanauj up to the banks of the Jamuna. They carried on hostilities against the Chedis as well as the Paramaras of Malwa, and raided Bihar and Bengal. Yasovarman's son Dhanga inflicted a defeat upon Govinda Chandra of Kanauj in A.D. 977, occupied Banaras by 988, led a campaign against the kingdom of Palas, and waged war against Andhra. His son Chanda bore the shock of Mahmud's attack.

The history of the Kalachuris of Tripuri, the Paramaras of Malwa, and the Chalukyas of Gujarat is a repetition of the same bloody tale of violence, expansion, decline. Nor do the kingdoms of Rajputana–Mewar of the Guhilas, Delhi of the Tomaras, Sakambhari of Chauhans show much variation.

In Kashmir the scandalous rule of Didda, one of the most unscrupulous and vicious queens ended with her death in A.D. 1003. Then the Lohara dynasty was established. Its first ruler Samgramaraja repelled the expeditions of Mahmud against Kashmir. But there was so much jealousy among the members of the royal family and disaffection among the officials and feudatories that Kashmir was never in a position to render any aid in the defence of India.

This narrative makes it clear that politically India in the eleventh century A.D. was so deeply absorbed in the internal contests of Hindu princes and chiefs that it was almost completely oblivious of the grave dangers lurking on the borders or actually besetting the north-western regions. Ferishta who wrote his history—**Gulshan-i-Ibrahimi**, in A.D. 1606, is the source of the information that Jaipal of the Hindu Shahiyah dynasty appealed to the Hindu kings of India and organised a league of Hindu rajas against Sabuktigin which included the Rajas of Delhi, Ajmer, and Kalinjar appears fanciful.

Delhi about the end of the tenth century A.D. was hardly more than a village under the petty Tomara chiefs who were probably feudatories of Pratiharas of Kanauj. Ajmer was founded by Ajayaraja in the first quarter of the twelfth century. Kalinjar was the capital of the Chandellas and Dhanga was then the ruler. He was confronted on the west by the Kachwahas who dispossessed him of Gwalior and on the east by the Palas whose province of Anga he was trying to annex. He was at the same time sending expeditions against Kanauj. It is difficult to believe that the Tomaras of Delhi, the Chaunas of Ajmer or the Chandellas of Kalinjar—none too well inclined towards one another, were able to spare contingents to march all the way to Afghanistan to help Jaipal. Such co-operation in the defence of a distant and almost unknown kingdom appears most unlikely, for neither to save such sacred places as Nagarkot, Thanesar, Mathura, or Somnath all situated within easy striking distance of neighbouring Hindu principalities, nor to resist the assaults on Kashmir, Kanauj, or Kalinjar—seats of important Hindu kingdoms, did any Raja make an attempt to rally together the forces of the Indian princes.

Mahmud was a soldier but no statesman. His hastily constructed empire was not founded upon any firm foundations, so within ten years of his death which took place in A.D. 1030, the whole of this jerry built structure fell to pieces. The Saljuqs took possession of its western parts, and the Indian princes occupied the country as far as the Satlej. In India only the Panjab remained under the rule of the Ghaznavids.

What was the effect of Mahmud's invasion? So far as the

conversion of the Hindus was concerned, Utbi and other Muslim scholars who wished to glorify Islam and demonstrate its superiority naturally give exaggerated accounts of conversions. Alberuni who worked in the Panjab with Brahman teachers and wrote his work on India in those times does not mention any mass conversions in the Panjab. The upper and lower Sindh seemed to possess large Hindu populations, which appears from the accounts of the Ismaili missionaries who carried on their activities in the 11th and 12th centuries, and of the Sufis in later times. It has been suggested that the majority of Sindhis adopted Islam under the Kalhoras and Talpurs. But this is not certain.

So far as the Panjab was concerned the indications are that it had still many non-Muslim inhabitants. The story of the treason of Nialtigin the Commander-in-Chief and the appointment of Tilak the Hindu officer with a Hindu force to punish him, and the pursuit of Nialtigin by the Jats "and every kind of infidel" on the banks of the Indus is a pointer. Again in Masud's campaign against the Saljuqs in Marv and in the battle of Dandanican the fact that the Hindu troops fought along with the Turks, Arabs and Kurds, is important.

What about the relations between the Hindus and the Muslims? Do they show the existence of a spirit of uncompromising animosity between them? Except the intemperate language used by the fanatical Ulama there do not appear to be many facts to substantiate it.

Did the ravages of the Ghazani tornado which uprooted dynasties and despoiled India of its collected treasures teach any lesson to the people of India? It has to be regretfully stated that the answer is in the negative. Arnold's lines express the real truth:

> The East bowed low before the blast,
> In patient, deep disdain.
> She let the legions thunder past
> And plunged in thought again.

An interval of one hundred and seventy-five years separates the sack of Somnath by Mahmud and the battle of Tarain which sealed the fate of Hindu India. The doom was unfortunately self-inflicted. There were numerous warnings of the impending crisis and the Indians had long enough time in which to set their house in order, but the Rajas took no heed. They continued the merry game of toppling one another, showing utter unconcern about happenings in the Panjab and beyond. Their lack of intelligence was abysmal. Although it need not have been so, for Muslim settlements dotted the whole country before the Ghorids fell upon their prey, in Banaras, Bahraich, Badaun, Kanauj, Unao and other places in Uttar Pradesh, in Hajipur and Maner in Bihar, in Rajputana, and all along the western coast from Kachh to Calicut. There were many settlements of Muslim merchants and missionaries from Turkistan, Khorasan, Arabia in India. Similarly Hindus and Buddhists were to be found in Central Asia, Afghanistan and farther west. The two together could have furnished all the information needed about developments in the Muslim lands. Apparently the need was not felt. Why? It is almost impossible to answer. Perhaps Alberuni found the secret when he described the Indian character in these words:

"They (the Hindus) believe that there is no country but theirs, no nation like theirs, no kings like theirs, no religion like theirs, no science like theirs. They are haughty, foolishly vain, self-conceited, and stolid....Their haughtiness is such that, if you tell them of any science or scholars in Khorasan and Persia, they will think you both an ignoramus and a liar. If they travelled and mixed with other nations, they would soon change their mind, for their ancestors were not as narrow minded as the present generation is."

"All their fanaticism is directed against those who do not belong to them—against all foreigners. They call them **Mlechha**, i.e., impure, and forbid having any connection with them by intermarriage or any other kind of relationship, or by sitting, eating and drinking with them, because thereby they think they would be polluted."[1]

This of course is true mainly of the Brahmans, with whom Al Biruni came into contact in his search for Indian sciences, philosophy and religion.

Whatever that may be, the fact remains that on the eve of the Muhammadan conquest the Hindu principalities were divided, engaged in never ending feuds and suicidal wars among themselves. In western India the Chalukyas, Paramaras and Chauhans fought with one another and also with their neighbours to the east and the south; in central India the Gohadvadas, Chandellas, Kalachuris, with some others thrown in, competed for supremacy; and in eastern India Palas and Senas of Bihar and Bengal were constantly under fire from Gahavadas of Kanauj and Gangas of Orissa.

Inevitably when the Ghurid hammer fell they were struck down one after another like nine pins. It is a matter for sorrow that religion proved a broken reed. It was incapable of eradicating the weaknesses of society, providing the bonds which could unite the diverse political units, or overcoming the forces—economic, social and political, which obstructed the consolidation of the people in a single organisation capable of resisting the foreigner's onslaught.

With the rapid conquest of India, which brought nearly the whole of the country under one rule in a little over a century, political conditions changed. Political changes in turn modified the economic conditions, although neither basically in the techniques of agriculture nor radically in the methods of industrial production. Social life came under the influence of the new rulers and profoundly affected culture. The settlements of the conquerors were largely confined to the towns and cities and places of strategical importance. The rural side felt the weight of their pressure much less.

The Ghurid conquest was not impelled by religious zeal; it was the sequence of the political developments in the Islamic

1 Sachaer, S.B.—Alberuni's India, pp. 19-23.

world. From Central Asia to Mesopotamia the newly formed Muslim states were locked in mortal combat against one another—the Buwaihids against the Saljuqs, the Saljuqs against the Khwarizmians. The Ghaznivids, Ghuzz and Ghurids were involved in this maelstrom and all were trembling for their very existence from the threat gathering in the east, from the Qara Khatais and the Mongols who soon irrupted into Central Asia and swept all of them away. As religion had failed to unite the Hindu principalities, equally so it failed to bind the Muslim sultanates together.

The Ghurids under Alauddin seized Ghazni and sacked it. They killed all the Muslims and burnt the city of Mahmud and earned the sobriquet of **Jahan Soz** (world burner). Occupation of territory in the north-west made the Ghurids turn to India where the Panjab was under the Ghaznavids and Multan under the Carmathians. They attacked them both and took possession of the Panjab and then only turned their attention to their Rajput neighbours whose mutual jealousies opened the gates wide in front of them.

Neither the Ghurids nor their successors the Mamluk Sultans did, however, pay much attention to theological principles or legal Codes of Islam in expanding their dominion in India or in organising their system of administration. Not the propagation of faith, but vaulting ambition, hunger for land, riches and power were the motives which actuated them. But while other warriors and administrators were mundane, the guardians of religion—priests, divines, Ulama, were deeply committed to cult, creed and law. There was unceasing debate between these two. Unfortunately although some Ulama were broadminded and realistic, many were narrow and bigoted literalists for whom the world was static. They wanted life to be congealed in the moulds of the first century of the Hijra.

Very often statesmen disregarded the counsel of these Ulama, but from time to time under economic and political stresses, and fear of loss of popularity, resistance weakened and misguided religious enthusiasm prevailed. But if we compare the record of occasional bigotry and fanaticism, which tarnishes the history of medieval India, with the tale of terrible persecutions and mass massacres which disgrace the pages of western history from the eighth century to the middle of the seventeenth, there is little doubt that the verdict will be greatly in favour of India.

It is interesting to institute a comparison between the theory of the Ulama and the practice of the monarchs. The theory of society and state according to the early jurists of Islam, whose authority whether followed in actual practice or not was always held in respect, was that society was a divine institution established for the purpose of achieving good life in this world and eternal happiness thereafter. The good life was life in accordance with the **Shariat** whose injunctions were based upon the **Quran,** the **Hadith** and the infallible authority of the consensus **(Ijma)** of the community **(Ummat)** which in practice meant the Ulama.

The necessity of the state arose because the **Shariat** had to be enforced and the laws relating to duties and prohibitions applied. The state functioned through the agency of the Caliphate, which constituted the supreme authority for the faithful all over the world. Muslims irrespective of colour, race or domicile formed one society, with the **Quran** as the sole authority for religion, and the Caliph as the one sovereign ruler binding all Muslims in one political body.

This theory finds elaborate exposition by Barni. By his time the authority of the Caliph had been replaced by that of the Sultan. This was the result of the historical developments in the Islamic world, according to which local chiefs had founded principalities which owed only nominal allegiance to the Caliph, and sometimes not even that, while the Caliph had become a puppet in the hands of powerful Sultans.

This situation affected the theory in the eleventh century. Ghazali held, "the function of government in the various lands is carried out by means of sultans, who owe allegiance to the Caliphate, Government in these days is a consequence solely of military power, and whosoever he may be to whom the possessor of military power gives his allegiance, that person is the Caliph."

Mawardi in his Ahkam-as-Sultaniyah went a step further and actually gave juristic recognition to the irregular states created by force. He categorised them as **Imarati Istila** (chieftancy by seizure). In India Barani upheld the highest claims of the sultanate. In the **Tarikh-i-Firozshahi** he defines the functions of the Sultan as two: **one**, protection of religion (**din panahi**) and **two**, maintenance and expansion of the realm (**Jahanbani** and **Jahangiri**). The first consisted of entertaining right beliefs, destruction of infidels and infidelity, eradication of corruption and inequity from the Muslims, patronage of the pious and the godly, discouragement of philosophers and rationalists, and establishment of justice. The second implied the provision of revenues, well equipped troops and well filled treasury and undertaking campaigns of conquest.

Barani, however, found that the first function was generally neglected by the Sultans. The sermons of Sayyid Nuruddin Mubarak Ghaznavi in the presence of Sultan Shamsud Din Iletmish went unheaded, and Balban used to tell repeatedly his sons, nephews and noblemen with tears in his eyes, "I am unable to perform the duty of the protection of the faith. Who am I that I should entertain the wish when none of my masters were able to fulfil the duty of the protection of religion."[1] He confessed that he could only perform the secular tasks of preventing injustice and maintenance of order.

When Qazi Mughith ud Din upbraided Alaud Din Khalji for neglecting the duties enjoined by the **Shariat**, his answer was that his actions were solely inspired by expediency and that he did not know that was required of him by the law of Islam. Barani himself admitted that it was not possible to rule India in accordance with the **Shariat**. He realised that the only

1 Ziaud Din Barni—*Tarikhi Firoz Shahi*, edited by Saiyid Ahmad Khan (Bibliotheca Indica edition), p. 44.

way to govern was by the regulations of the state, (**zawabit**). He declared: "A state regulation (**zabita**) in the technique of administration means a rule of action which the king has imposed as an obligatory duty upon himself for realising the welfare of the State, and from which he absolutely never deviates."[1]

Apparently the Sultans of the early Middle Ages, while paying lip service to canonical theories looked upon themselves as monarchs independent of the Caliph and deriving their authority directly from God. Minhajud Din Siraj gives the title of **Zill Allah Fil Alamin** to Iltuttmish, **Sayah i Yazdan** to Nazir ud Din Mahmud and Balban. Amir Khusrau speaks of Kaiqubad as **Sayah-i-Yazdani Pak.** Qutubud Din Mubarak Shah called himself **Khalifatal Allah.** The Mughal Emperors completely repudiated the Khilafat, which had been forcibly seized by the Ottoman Sultans, and assumed the titles of **Khalifatal Allah, Zillah Allah** and **Vakil Allah.**

Abul Fazl states the theory of Mughal kingship in these words: Royalty is a light emanating from God. and a ray from the sun, the illuminator of the universe, the argument of the book of perfection, the receptacle of all virtues. Modern thought calls this light **Farri izidi** (the divine light), and the tongue of antiquity called it **Kiyan Khura** (the sublime halo). It is communicated by God to kings without the intermediate assistance of any one, and men, in the presence of it, bend the forehead of praise towards the ground of submission."[2]

Aurangzeb was described as Sultan of India, Commander and Imam of the Faithful, Stay and Support of the Musalmans, and Warrior on the Path of God, by Shaikh Muhammad al-Muradi (d. 1791) the chief Hanafi Mufti of Damascus. The titles bestowed on him indicate the great distance the theory of the

1 Habib M. and Khan, A.U.S.—*The Political Theory of the Delhi Sultanate,* translation of Barni's *Fatwa-i-Jahandari,* p. 64.

2 Abul Fazl Allami: *The Ain-i-Akbari,* translated by H. Blochmann, 2nd edition, p. 3.

Caliphate had travelled since its inception. In regarding Aurangzeb as **Amir ul Mominir**, it formulated a claim at which the emperor who was an extreme stickler for the **Shariat** would have blushed.

Nevertheless these facts make it abundantly clear that the Muslim rulers of India were not animated by the desire to establish a state in accord with the juristic principles of Islam, but were generally guided in their administration by political expediency. The sanctimonious scholars, however, shut ostrich-like their eyes and chose to believe that their Muslim kings were pious and dedicated followers of the **Shariat.** Unfortunately, as they had the near monopoly of scholarship they not only kept themselves under illusion they have continued to mislead their uncritical readers throughout the ages.

Minds have been so much affected by this approach that almost every political movement in India is indiscriminately ascribed to religion whether the facts fit the theory or not. The Maratha armies are regarded as symbols of Hindu resurgence although they did not spare the Rajputs, the Bengalis, the Tanjoreans and the Hindus of the Doab. The Sikhs are made the champions of the Brahman and the cow although they despoiled many petty Hindu hill states. The Jats whose alliances and counter-alliances were based on their fluctuating interests and who made no distinction between Hindu and Muslim chiefs, have been represented as the defenders of the Hindu community, in spite of the fact that they did not lift their little finger to defend Mathura and Brindaban when Ahmad Shah Abdali rained fire and brimstone on the hapless cities.

If then neither the Hindus nor the Muslims were actuated principally by religious motives in their politics how is one to account for and judge the undoubted acts of vandalism perpetrated throughout the long period of the Middle Ages—the massacre of men, the immolation of women, the spoliation of places of worship, the forced conversions, the imposition of capitation tax? In explanation, I must say that there is no such thing as a just or righteous aggressive war. At the same time, it must be admitted sorrowfully that no period of human history has been free from incidents of large scale cruelty, manslaughter, arson and destruction in a myriad shape. War is a pest from which humanity has suffered in all countries and at all times. It has caused widespread misery, imposed unbearable indignity and dishonour, and deeply wounded the spirit of man, and even today it hangs like the sword of Damocles over the devoted head of man. No plea can ever make it right. Unfortunately if the vanquisher and the aggressor are undoubtedly to blame, it is difficult to absolve completely the vanquished and the victims from the charge of constructive complicity.

War has always tended to be brutal, even twentieth century wars between highly civilized nations were accompanied with bombing and burning of towns, destruction of hospitals, schools and churches. In the ruder middle ages when no international laws or conventions existed and intercourse between peoples was rare and those who met in the field of battle were utter strangers and therefore without pity or compassion, inspired only by mutual fear and hatred, it is not surprising that ravaging of territory, killing and enslaving of men and women should have been regarded legitimate. If we put beside the happenings in India, the terrible events of the wars of Charlemagne in the eighth century, of the Norman conquest of Britain in the eleventh, of the Thirty Years War of Europe in the seventeenth and of the first and second World Wars in the twentieth, it will not be difficult to decide which entailed greater suffering and barbarity.

Granting then that the Turkish invaders during the course of fighting committed inhuman outrages and intolerable atrocities, what happened when armed conflict ceased and the victors settled down to carry on the work of administration? Were the relations between the rulers and the ruled such as to perpetuate opposition and hatred, or did they find ways of living together and co-operating in the tasks of peace? Al Biruni's quotation given above seems to suggest the worst. What he reports may have been true of Brahmans, who in any case were a very exclusive group. They had little social intercourse with the other Hindus because of the taboos regarding marriage and dining, and also because of their superior status and limited sphere of activities. But it is not borne out by history.

There is another side to the picture. The Hindus apparently had little hesitation in co-operating with the Muslims in many fields. Mahmud and Masud had Hindu officers and soldiers in their armies. The Gukkhars and Jats who were warlike Hindu tribes of the Panjab took service under whosoever promised them opportunities of fight and loot. They formed part of many Muslim armies. In a Sanskrit inscription of 1328 A.D. one Khwaja Jalal Uddin Khoja, governor of the ancient Chedi-country in the Madhya Pradesh, mentions Hindu military officers of Sultan Muhammad and a Muslim officer Hisamuddin Shafiq (Hisamadini Chhipaka) commanding the Hindu Kharpara troops of the royal army.

From the Purusa Pariksa of Vidyapati Thakur (15th century) it appears that Hindu princes Narsimha and Charchika Deva fought for Muhammad bin Tughlak against the Raja of Kampila in Telangana who had espoused the cause of the rebel Bahauddin Gurshasp cousin of the Sultan. The case of Himu the general of Muhammad Adil Shah Sur who offered battle to Akbar at Panipat is well-known. Of the Mughal Emperors and their Hindu mansabdars and military leaders it is not necessary to say anything, and even school boys know of them.

The employment of Hindus in the military forces was not an unavoidable necessity, but it was done because loyalty was not in those times regarded as inseparable from religion. But the appointment of Hindus in civil departments specially finance was essential. It was not possible for foreigners unacquainted with the languages of the country and its administrative and financial system—especially the land revenue system on which the economy of the state was based, to dispense with the services of the old staff. Evidently the members of the lower staff were mostly Hindus, but even from the higher offices Hindus were not altogether excluded. But in a predominantly militarily oriented state it was inevitable that the higher services should be manned with the kith and kin of the ruling class. It should, however, be remembered that a large fraction of government, namely, local government in rural areas, was in the hands of Hindu chiefs and landlords, and they were not altogether a submissive or peaceful lot. History is replete with stories of their contumacy and defiance. Strong and energetic Sultans alone were able to keep these Hindus in order.

In the early Middle Age from Muhammad bin Qasim to Adil Shah Sur names of high Hindu officials are met with. They are not in large numbers as in the Mughal Empire, but are not conspicuous by their absence. Some of them have been mentioned earlier, others were—Buchand a high official of finance department under Alaud Din Khalji; Rajani, Hathiya and Birnathan Kotwal under later Mamluk Sultans, Nain under Jalaluddin Khalji, his son Dusaju under Alaud Din, Ghiyas ud Din Tughlaq and Muhammad Tughlaq. Samar Singh Jain the **Vyavahar** (agent or commissioner) of Qutubud Din Mubarak Shah and Ghiyas ud Din, and later the governor of Telingana, Saiju, a minister in the Benaras Raj, who accepted service under Sultan Muhammad.

When the Mughal Empire was founded, its enlightened rulers followed the wise policy of throwing open their highest services to the Hindus. The names of Man Singh, Todar Mal, Ray Rayan Raghunath, Jaswant Singh and Jai Singh are household words. Even Shivaji was the recipient of the title of Raja and his son Sambhaji of a mansab of 5,000 from Aurangzeb, and in later times the Peshwas Baji Rao and Balaji Baji Rao were appointed Deputy Viceroys of Malwa. Madhoji Sindhia became the **Naib Vakil** of the Peishwa who was given the office of **Vakil.** The Rajas of Jaipur, Jodhpur and Bikaner were on the service rolls of the Mughals.

These are facts which negate the theory that the two communities lived constantly growling at one another and with daggers drawn all the time. It is unfortunate that when these relations are under consideration the vast masses are completely forgotten. The fact is that so far as the humbler peoples were concerned—artisans, craftsmen, peasants, traders, labourers, whether they were Hindu or Muslim, there was little competition or conflict among them for the simple reason that they were organised into occupational groups or castes and therefore did not tread on one another's toes. They lived together in the villages and towns and on the whole peacefully. All the fuss and fluster affected the microscopic minority of the upper classes—the privileged groups.

But even among them as the record of military and civil services shows there was willingness to co-operate. There are numerous records attesting to the goodwill and appreciation of the Muslim rulers by the Hindus which prove that there was no settled antagonism between them. Bhanukara describes Sher Shah as (क्षि ति प कु ल म णि) **Kshitipakulamani**—the jewel of the Kingly race. Govind Bhatta Akbariya addresses the Emperor in these words:

शार्दूलोऽसि प्रकोष्ठे मदकल-करटी मांसल स्कंध कूटे दोः। स्तम्भे नागराजो
ध्वनिषु जलधरः केसरी मध्यदेशे। धम्मिले ध्वान्त-धारा मनसि जलनिधि
भ्रूयुगे कालदण्डः तत्सयुं श्री हुमायुं-कुल-तिलकमणे भीषणाद् भीषणोऽसि॥

"You are a tiger in regard to your fore arm; a fleshy intoxicated elephant in regard to your shoulder; as regards your two arms a noble elephant; as regards voice a cloud; a lion in regard to your waist; your sword blade is jet black like a braid; your mind is the ocean; your eye-brows the staff of death; o! scion of the family of Humayun, it is true that you are more terrible than the terrible one (**Yama**)."

Jagananatha Panditaraja eulogises Jahangir thus:

श्यामं यज्ञोपवीतं तव किमिनि मषी-संगमात् कुत्र जालः। सोऽयं शीतांशु-
कन्या-पयसि कथमभूत्तज्जलं कज्जलाक्तम्। व्याकृप्यन्नूरदीन-क्षितिरमण-रिपु
क्षोणिभृत पक्ष्मसाक्षो लाक्षा क्षीणाक्षु-धारा-सभुदित-सरिता सर्वतः संगमेन॥

"Why is your sacred thread black? On account of its contact with ink. Wherefrom has that come? From the waters of thé Narbada. How did its water become collyrium? On account of its union with the rivers from all round originating in the ceaseless flow of tears of lacs of beautiful ladies with long eye-lashes belonging to the hostile court of the wrathful king Nuruddin."

And of Shah Jahan he writes:

दिल्लीश्वरो वा जगदीश्वरो वा मनोरथान् पुरयितुं समर्थः। अन्यैर्न्टंपासैः परिदीयमानं शाकाय वा स्याल्लवणाय वा स्यात्।

"It is the Lord of Delhi or the Lord of universe who is capable of fulfilling desires. The other rulers are able to give either a vegetable or salt."

All the misunderstanding between the Hindus and Muslims was really confined to sections of the Ulama on the one side and of the Pandits on the other. Among the Ulama whose books constituted their whole world there was inordinate pride of race, religion and conquest and among the Pandits immersed in their other worldly scholarship there was complete indifference towards the foreigners and their culture and a sense of superiority of their own philosophy and faith. They were the moulders of minds. Them have we to thank for the damnosa hereditas which brought about the partition of this impartible land consecrated by a millennium of living together, deeply involved in a common destiny. It is necessary now to shake off the fatal grip of these old men of the mountain and allow the fresh breezes of freedom, understanding and amity to dissipate the miasma of the evil inheritance.

3

INDIA IN THE MODERN AGE

On June 23, 1757, a small army consisting of 1,022 European soldiers and artillerymen and 2,100 Indian sepoys trained on the European model, was deployed by their none-too-confident commander Clive on to the rain-sodden plain of Plassey. Against him was arrayed the 50,000 strong force of Siraj-ud-Daula, the young, arrogant and impetuous, but pusillanimous, Nawab of Bengal. The sight of the proud bearing and glittering accoutrements of the enemy was not exactly calculated to spur the resolution of the hesitant British commander to fight. Nevertheless the two blundered into a skirmish.

The morning had been occupied by a desultory cannonade in which both sides took part. But as soon as the sun began to travel towards the western horizon, the Nawab's troops started falling back to their camp. Clive was enjoying his afternoon Siesta, according to the contemporary historian, Orme. His second in command, taking courage in both hands, gave the order to advance upon the retreating forces of the Nawab on his own responsibility. The Indian side had no stomach for a real fight, for in the words of Clive "tricks, chicanery, intrigues, politics and the Lord knows what" had settled the issue before the death of the only loyal captain convinced the Nawab that discretion was the better part of the valour. He incontinently fled to his capital, and there met with his doom.

This sorry episode, none too creditable either for the victors or the vanquished, described as 'the greatest anti-climax in all history', opened a new chapter in the long and vicissitudinous history of relations between the East and the West. Plassey marked the rise of the sun of a new civilisation which arose above the horizon of the Atlantic and whose refulgence paled the stars of Asia into insignificance.

The shattering event throws out a challenge to the historian. India's dismal failure and England's resounding triumph call for explanation. For Plassey was not a mere military defeat, it was the debacle of a whole civilisation. The victory was not due to military superiority alone, although it is true that the British six-pounders were better served than the huge calibred twenty-four to thirty-pounder guns of Siraj-ud-Daula. Was it lack of courage? Indian troops have proved on a thousand battlefields before and since Plassey that they are inferior to none so far as the possession of martial spirit is concerned.

Seeley testifies, "the Nations of India have been conquered by an army of which, on the average, about a fifth part English. In the early battles of the Company by which its power was decisively established at the seige of Arcot, at Plassey, at Buxar, there seems always to have been more sepoys than Europeans on the side of the Company. And, let us observe further, that we do not hear of the sepoys fighting ill or of the English bearing the whole brunt of the conflict."[1]

The British troops were indeed better trained and disciplined, but tactics could be learnt, as the Marathas and the Sikhs demonstrated in later wars. Yet possession of modern weapons and the use of modern methods of warfare proved un-

1 Seeley, J.—Expansion of England—pp. 300-302.

availing to them, and within a hundred years of Plassey the whole of India had passed under British dominion.

The fact is that Clive and his thousand European soldiers represented a new way of life which the West had forged in the centuries preceding their advent to India. In the middle of the 18th century, Europe, and especially its most advanced member, Britain, had become the bearer of a dynamic, expansive culture. During the last five hundred years it had undergone several revolutions which had broken the bonds of medievalism and feudalism. They had emancipated the individual and society from static ways of life—the rigid social hierarchy, the stifling domination of the Church, the pernicious economy of the feudal agrarian system, the political tyranny of the aristocracy. First had come the economic revolution of the English boroughs and the continental communes, which promoted trade and industry, supported the accumulation of capital, encouraged urban autonomy and brought into being the middle class, the principal agency of all subsequent economic, social and political change.

In the homes of this class, in the cities of Italy first and then of the other European lands, there came a marvellous awakening of the spirit—a liberation of the mind from the shackles of authority, an opening of the eye to the unknown realms of nature and an insight into the inner resources of the mind. Man had found himself. Self-authorized, self-dependent, self-assured, free, he faced the world which he went out to conquer. He crosses the oceans and bestrode the continents. Poor, the untold riches of the world were spread out before him; short of food, an unlimited vista of fertile lands invited him to settle and exploit. If densely-populated, old Europe offered 24 acres for the support of each individual, the empty spaces of the new world across the Atlantic placed at his disposal an area four to five times as large. It has been calculated that before the great discoveries of the 16th century, the population of Europe was about one hundred million souls, and the land at their disposal three million, seven hundred and fifty square miles. The quantity of gold and silver available was about two hundred million dollars. At the time the battle of Plassey was fought, the population had registered an increase of over 50 per cent, the area of land had multiplied by six, but the stock of precious metals had risen by 2,000 per cent. How much had been added to wealth of commodities, there is no means of ascertaining.

The breezes that wafted Europe's ships to and fro the Atlantic created a boom in its economy. They also filled the nostrils with the breath of the frontier spirit—self-reliance, resourcefulness, ruthlessness, contempt for tradition and authority.

On the heels of the Renaissance and the Age of Discovery came the Reformation. The universalism which the Roman Catholic Church had sought to impose upon the Christian peoples of Europe carried with it implications galling to the new sense of independence which was emerging. Both interest and principle, politics and faith, dictated a repudiation of Papal authority, an affirmation of freedom from foreign control of religious establishments. The movement stimulated both the growth of capitalism and individualism.

Then followed the political revolution of 1688 in England. It was an important link in the chain of events which transformed the political system of England. It made Parliament the centre round which the life of the people revolved. More, Hobbes' prophetic vision was justified, Austin's definition foreshadowed. The Leviathan, the omni-competent power, the sovereign State, had come into being. The bearer of its person was Parliament, its sustainer the middle class—the merchant turned landlord, the landlord became a shareholder in the monopolist joint stock company of merchant adventures. From the seeds sown during the Puritan Revolution a mighty tree had grown—its fruits were liberty, fortune, due process of law, above all, national consciousness.

The age of nationalism had been ushered in. In 1740, the first national hymn, 'Rule, Britania, Britania rule the waves', had been composed. National opinion was voiced through ten million copies of newspapers. Bolingbroke expatiated upon the spirit of patriotism. Milton in his stately prose celebrated the birth of the new Israel, the new England, 'a Nation of Prophets, of Sages, and of Worthies'.

Another revolution with even more far-reaching consequences was trickling through. Jethro Tull, 'Turnip' Townsend, Robert Bakewell were the pioneers of an agrarian movement which was soon to merge itself in the mighty flood of the Industrial Revolution.

The prophets of this age in which man and nature had assumed a new significance were Locke, Newton, Hume and Adam Smith. They provided the justification for the social and political changes of the times and laid the theoretic foundations of English culture. They determined the framework for thought and discovered the laws, processes and methods of its activity. In their philosophy, man and nature stand face to face as two independent principles. Experience correlates man—the private independent conscious substance, with nature—an objective and public order of material atoms. Experience is individual and creates the private world of knowledge, and in this all individuals are alike. Hence follow equality and liberty, absence of constraint in religion and minimization of constraint in society, politics and economics. Man is a free being who creates his social and political structures, gives laws to himself and measures out the things that are in heaven and on earth.

Nature is a unified order functioning in objective time and space. It writes on the clean slate of man's consciousness; man reads the signs and combines them and the book of forms, sounds and odours is compiled, and while Nature is one, the books are as many as men.

The revolution—tossed civilization of the West is like the Heraclitean river in which one cannot step twice. Change is its essential character. Its intellectual basis is that restless knowledge whose prior and posterior are always in flux. Einstein averred, "Our notions of physical reality can never be final.

Its interest in things which are not seen but are eternal is overlaid by its preoccupation with things which throng and press upon the senses". A modern American thinker points out, 'We believe our Western scientific, philosophical, and religious theories to be true not because we directly introspect or sense what they assert, but because, assuming them by hypothesis to be true, it follows by logical deduction or mathematical calculation that the empirical facts which are directly sensed or introspected should be what "they are".'

In the tropical mango grove of Plassey, as Clive nervously surveyed the field on that wet summer day, did he perhaps subconsciously realise that he was the instrument of irresistible destiny? Opposite to him stood serried ranks which presented a glittering facade. But what lay behind it? A civilization over three thousand years old, which had suffered from the inconstancy of fortunate. Noontides of glory, had alternated with long dusks of internal strife and dark nights of humiliation. Invaders had come, conquered, built empires, established peace, given opportunity to wealth to accumulate, arts to flourish and culture to refine. Aliens had entered with strange religions and unknown ways. Most of them became absorbed in the spongy softness of Hindu society. Islam retained its religious individuality although cultural exchange profoundly modified it; so much so that Babur, the founder of the Mughal Empire, was struck by the wide differences between the peoples of India, including his co-religionists, and the peoples of other lands. He was constrained to distinguish their culture by designating it 'the Hindustani way'.

Babur's Empire waxed, its reputation spread far and wide, Milton sang of 'the wealth of Ormuz and of Ind'. European travellers who visited the country found that Delhi and Agra surpassed London and Paris in population and wealth. Akbar, Jahangir and Shahjahan raised India to the pinnacle of fame. Then the wheel turned. The edifice of the great Empire was shaken. In the 18th century it lay in ruins. The central authority which sustained order and unity lost its virtue, and India was turned into a human cauldron of seething and warring elements, a true exemplar of the Hobbesian state of nature'.

Destruction of the gentile plant of political loyalty gave free rein to unprincipled self-seeking. Destruction of political unity impoverished the state and spread economic chaos. Each one for himself and the devil take the hindmost, became the general maxim of conduct. But such a political crash was not altogether unprecedented. A number of times before similar anarchic situations had occurred. They were followed by reconstruction either by some power within the country or by a conqueror from abroad. But the new structure which arose on the ruins of the old did not alter the ground plan. Social system, economy and culture continued from age to age without any revolutionary or basic change.

The British conquest of India did not conform to this pattern. The encounter between two fundamentally different civilizations was a novel experience and it had fateful consequences.

Plassey threw out an unprecedented challenge to the traditionist India, but her defences did not hold. The tide of Western culture crossed the bar and came flooding into the land. Much of the accumulated stinking debris of ages was swept away and with it a considerable lot that was sound and healthy also. But historical catastrophies like their natural counterparts do not stop to choose and discriminate.

Immediately after the conquest a chain reaction started. It gathered amazing speed. Europe had traversed the interval from the medieval to the modern in 500 years. Half a dozen revolutions had marked the stages of its progress: three economic revolutions–commercial, agrarian and industrial, a cultural revolution–the Reformation; and a political revolution–the English, which established Parliamentary rule, and the French which swept away the ancient regime. They culminated in establishing the modern national sovereign state by the end of the 18th century.

India made a similar journey from medievalism to modernism, and the route passed through similar stages, but instead of five it took India only a century and half to travel the distance. It was as a result of economic, social and political revolutions that India which was a loose conglomeration of autonomous semi-independent village republics held together by slender ties of an overall suzerain authority became a united independent sovereign nation, the second largest State of the modern world.

In the process of East going West, there have been varying degrees of willing acceptance, deliberate rejection and all the shades of submission, conscious and unconscious co-operation, imitation and assimilation. The West had transmitted itself sometimes in the form of force and prestige, sometimes as example and persuasion, and sometimes as sheer necessity. The process has been in operation since Plassey.

The process started on the economic plans. It struck down the isolation, self-sufficiency and organic unity of the village. In place of the agrarian system of which the free peasant cultivator, the real producer of wealth, was the permanent limb; the intermediary a casual participant in his productive processes and a collector of rents for the State; and the State a more or less sleeping partner in the rural economy, entirely new schemes were introduced. According to one scheme a hereditary class of landlords was created, and the cultivator was reduced to the position of a tenant-at-will. The landholder became the owner of the land and acquired the proprietory rights of gift, mortgage and sale. Under another scheme—the ryotwari, the state became the landlord and the cultivator a holder of usufructuary tenure.

Land tended to become a marketable commodity in either case. This tendency was reinforced by the injection of money into the agrarian system. Rent and revenue were no longer linked to the amount of produce from crop to crop, but were realised in cash. They were not dependent upon the quantum of produce, but were fixed in cash for long periods of time. Failure to pay was punishable with ejectment and the sale of the land. The new system of landholding broke up the ancient collectivist organization. The dealings of the state with the landlord and the tenant emphasized the responsibilities of the individual. Money encouraged functionless absentee landlordism. But this class became more like the French rentier than the English squire, only unlike the French, their income was not derived from stocks and securities, but from land. They congregated in towns, built Western-looking homes with Western furniture, imitated the manners of the Western ruling class, sent their children to English schools or to England, and were regarded as the pillars of the Empire. They showed the attributes of a middle class—a class between the foreign ruling oligarchy and the Indian masses, a class interested in money and the advantages which its possession conferred—influence in society and in government largely exercised to promote class interests.

The cultivator lost the protection of the old village system and poor and resourceless was thrown into the maelstrom of competition. Payments of rents in money forced his produce into the market, dominated by grain merchants and moneylenders. This encouraged the transfer of land from the genuine agriculturist to the urban land speculator. Money gave an impetus to the increase of money crops. No longer was immediate consumption the objective of production. Specialisation of crops grew and an ever-widening market swept the village products into its cavernous bosom to satisfy its insatiable appetite.

Two factors had their impact upon the village—the introduction of the Western means of transport and communication, and the growth of population. The British built new roads and bridges and improved the old ones, and in 1854 laid the first railway lines. Telegraphs followed. Together they gave an immense impetus to the mobility of man and of goods. Peace and order and the elimination of some of the Malthusian factors inhibitive of growth pushed up population. It grew from less than 150 millions in the 18th century to over 200 millions in 1872. with the result that land came under short supply and man became overabundant. While in the Deccan in 1771 the average holding of a peasant had an area of 40 acres, in 1818 it was reduced to 17½ acres, and in 1915 to seven acres.[1]

In the absence of alternative avenues of employment, pressure upon land enormously increased, the urge for movement was accentuated, and the old isolation completely broke down. Conditions promoting the economic unification of the vast subcontinent were established. The creation of a highly-centralised system of government in which minute details of administration were controlled from the capital and all areas were brought under the rigid frame of uniform impersonal laws, gave powerful support to this tendency.

In the sphere of trade and industry, the change was equally radical. Village industry was shattered, because it could not withstand the double shock of measures of protection adopted by the English Government for its own home products and the competition of the fast developing factory system of England. The handloom was no match for the powerloom, and the poor village weaver had no shield against the selfishness of a commercially-minded imperialist power. England needed raw materials for her growing industry and a market for the disposal of manufactured goods. India's extensive arable lands and rapidly-increasing population fulfilled both needs. So, India's economy was geared to that of Britain. A vast field for the investment of British capital was opened. A commercial revolution weighed anchor. Eventually, it landed India squarely into the world market, with its mechanism of price adjustment and its economic consequences.

The landed middle class was swelled by the addition of a mercantile section, which soon became dissatisfied with its somewhat secondary and subordinate role and began to clamour for opportunities to utilize its capital to share the profits of large-scale industry. But their opportunities were slow to materialise and the Indian industrial revolution awaited the dawn of a better day.

---

1 Harold Mann, *The Deccan Village*.

The destruction of village industry compelled the artisan either to join the army of landless labourers in the rural areas or to migrate to towns. Either alternative provided grist to the mill of common discontent.

The agrarian and commercial revolution demolished the walls which divided Indians into atomised groups. New production techniques, new means of transport and communication and new methods of economic transaction combined with new ways of government and administration provided the neural processes which began to link the independent groups inhabiting India to form an organic whole. As the body was being built up, the spirit of a new social order was making ready to enter.

This was the spirit of modernism, of which the intellectual revolution, the religious and social reform movement, the literary renaissance and the artistic efflorescence were manifestations. It changed Indian traditional attitudes towards man and nature, and brought about a transformation of old values.

But of all the developments—technical, economic, social and political, the emergence of the new individual was the most significant. For through him, through his love embracing all his countrymen, his identification of his individual self with the collective self of India, his realisation that self-fulfilment was identical with the service of his people and that progress towards freedom could only be achieved by sacrifice, the new India was born. The uniquenesses and the universality of the individual had acquired new dimensions.

The history of modern India is then the saga of this transformation of the individual—in status and in character, and I propose in this part of my discourse to deal with this all absorbing theme.

According to all philosophies and psychologies—except the most extreme like the Materialist and the Behaviourist, man is a compound of two parts. One part is the eternal and universal principle, described as the absolute, the noumenal, the transcendental and the spiritual. The other is the conditioned, which is bound by the categories of time, space and causation. It is relative, phenomenal and material. Indian philosophy calls them Purusha and **Prakriti, Atman** and **Maya.**

Human intellect has so far failed to unravel their exact relationship. Vedanta regards the situation indescribable (anirvachaniya). For relation implies both identity and difference. But what is identical between the two it is hard to tell although the differences are easy to describe.

The absolute is simple, self-conscious, self-illumined, independent; it is the conscious element which carries within it the principle of self-consciousness. The relative, on the other hand, is complex, phenomenal, activated and illumined by the other part and dependent upon it. It is constituted of sheaths, material, biological, physiological, and mental involving feeling, willing and knowing. They veil the light which is the spirit.

The association of the two—the unmoved mover and the moved, is responsible for the strange drama which is human life—individual and collective. The association provides the drive which urges human evolution from savagery to civilisation, from bondage to the natural and the material to freedom, and from ignorance to self knowledge.

The evolution is a twofold process, inner and outer, individual and collective, spiritual and intellectual as well as social and material. It implies a growing self-illumination of consciousness, a broadening of the area of human relations, a deepening and purification of emotions, an advance of knowledge and the conquest of nature. Every culture endeavours to discover means by which the involvement of the spirit in the phenomenal and the physical brings about the realisation of the perfection of both the parts. Religion, social order, economic and political organisation all serve as means to the supreme end of the individual, namely, perfection.

Now ancient Indian culture conceived of perfection in terms of right knowledge, right feeling and right action, but considered knowledge as basic. It inferred from the duality of man's nature that knowledge must be of two kinds—the knowledge of the absolute or the transcendental and the knowledge of the relative or the phenomenal. The first is known as Para Vidya, and the second Apara.

This duality became incorporate in culture and determined all values of life. But the higher value was assigned to transcendental knowledge and both the individual and society aimed at its acquisition and co-operated in its quest. The perfect individual contributed to the perfection of society and the social order provided the necessary conditions for the perfection of the individual.

In the search for the absolute India tended to ignore the world which was subject to change, and to hold all that related to this world as inferior.

The perfect man was above name and form for he had transcended all that was particular, and had become one with the universal. Because of this attitude, particular men and women were regarded as non-entities. For instance, we know almost nothing about the seers who composed the Vedas, the Upanishads, and the whole of the Vedic literature, and as little about the Buddha and Mahavira. The great literary geniuses like Kalidasa, Bhavabhuti; philosophers like Gotama, Kannada, Badarayana; scientists of the calibre of Charaka, Susruta, Varahamihira and Panini are mere names. Even the great men of action who played historical roles are figures of myth and legend, e.g., Chandra Gupta Maurya, Asoka, Chandragupta Vikramaditya, Samudragupta, Pulekesin and Rajaraja Chola. Their anonymity undoubtedly negates egoism, and by the same token exalts their achievement.

The pursuit of the ideal of atonement or of unity in diversity, and of the true, the real and the good in the fleeting, ever-changing world, inspired every aspect of culture—art, literature, the organisation of social order—the fourfold division into classes, and the structure of the state.

But the very virtues of the culture proved its undoing. The dualism in ideas assumed inflexibility; the dichotomy of society—the Dwija against the rest, created insuperable barriers between the classes; the division between the ruling and the ruled brought about the polarization of rights and duties and disrupted the sense of identity and loyalty. In the words of Tagore, "Formalism, often unjust, often tyrannical grew at the expense of freedom of thought. The tenets of conduct which Manu had laid down hardened into time honoured traditions."[1]

The fragmentation of society was stereotyped in the caste socially, the isolated village economically, and the tribal principality politically. India in the ancient times was thus like Europe in the later middle ages. Both had a common religion, a common learned language and a common culture, but both were completely pulverised into fragments socially and politically.

Hindu culture by confining the freedom of the individual to matters spiritual, unfortunately denied him independence in every other sphere of life. So although it continued to flourish fitfully with many interludes of threatened disruption till the end of the tenth century, at last its sun began to set. Lack of inner harmony and tragic inability to evolve a consolidated all-India society and polity rendered it unfit to resist the onslaught of the peoples knocking at the gate.

The Turk and Tartar hordes poured out from Central Asia. They brought with them a new religion, and a different culture—both moulded by the genius of Iran, and carrying in their subconscious mind suppressed memories of their contacts with the Hindu and Buddhist cultures of old. Their religion and culture had mixed elements of other worldliness and temporal interests. But they gave to the latter much greater value than Ancient India. They assigned equal importance to the individual's duties as a spiritual as well as a worldly being.

Their religion—Islam, exalted individualism. It asserted the equality of all men. It made each one responsible for his deeds and for his ultimate destiny. It discarded the idea of a

---

1 Crisis in Civilisation.

saviour as intermediary between God and man. It laid great stress upon belief and obedience to the will of God as declared through the Prophet Muhammad. According to it not reason but intuition and feeling were the basis of man's relation to Allah. This feeling aspect of faith was greatly emphasized by the mystics of Islam—the Sufis. As feeling by its very nature is individualistic, unlike reason which is universalistic, Muslim culture inevitably laid much stress upon the dignity and worth of the individual.

This may be illustrated by the analysis of various aspects of Indo-Islamic culture, in practical life as well as in thought. Take for instance history:

We know a great deal more about the lives of the men of action of the Middle Ages than those of ancient times. The Sultans of Delhi—Balban, Alaud Din Khalji, Muhammad bin Tughlak are no dim legendary figures. Babar, Jahangir, Shahjahan and Aurangzeb are men of well pronounced individuality whose peculiarities of character are writ large on the canvas of history.

Equally was the stamp of individuality impressed on every aspect of medieval culture, on the arts—architecture, painting and music, and literature where the authors—poets, historians, letter writers, were well-known both as men and stylists. But it was in the realm of religion that individualism manifested itself clearly. The intellectual and interpretational differences among the Ulama (the doctors of theology) and the proliferation of orders among the Sufis (mystics) was an expression of the new tendency. The Chishtiah, Qadiriya, Suhravardiya, Kabrawiya, Naqshbandiya and other disciplines had their own peculiarities—in practice and belief.

Nor was the movement confined to the Muslims. The Hindu culture of the Middle Ages was profoundly influenced by this new emphasis on the individual. The great Acharyas of the early middle age—Sankara, Ramanuja, Madhwa, and Vallabha, are much less elusive figures, and the promulgators of the Bhakti movements—Nirguna (unconditioned and absolute) and Saguna (personalistic), are men and women of flesh and blood whose careers and teachings bear the impress of personality.

The same remark applies to the literary geniuses of the times—Sur, Tulasi, Biharilal, Deva, Rahim and Malik Muhammad Jayasi, in Hindi, and the numerous poets in the literary regional languages whose development was fostered by Muslim rulers.

Even the Hindu caste notwithstanding its rigidities felt the loosening effect of the spirit of the age. Most of the Nirguna Bhaktas repudiated caste. A considerable number among them belonged to lower castes and even outcastes. The very fact that in the north the Kshatriyas had ceased to be rulers and Brahmanas had consequently lost the status of mentors of princes had a profound effect upon the Hindu social system. The Vaisyas and Sudras began to live in a freer atmosphere and castes of Kayasthas and Banias acquired a special social status in the service of the state.

Medieval India had travelled far from the ancient times in spirit, in thought, in social life and manners. Medieval man was less bound to the chariot wheels of authority and was more assertive.

In the eighteenth century the tide of energism—spiritual and temporal, began to ebb. The spirit of adventure which inspired both seekers after God and men of action became bogged in the quagmire of internecine conflicts, shortsighted egoistic enterprises, repudiation of loyalties which raise the individual above his immediate petty concerns. Life became irresponsible, morals corrupt. The pursuit of fleeting whims and satisfaction of sensual urges, in other words, the overmastering tyranny of hunger and sex established its sway over the Indian mind. The slavery to passion within prepared the ground for slavery from without, which fastened itself upon the prostrate body of India in the shape of British imperialism.

The conquest of India which was initiated on the mango

grove of Plassey was essentially a collision between two opposite cultures. It threatened a total 'boulversement' of Indian culture. But although the negative of the West impinged upon and destroyed much of what was stereotyped, decadent and traditional, in the process it released the powers of independent and creative activity. The dialectics of progress ushered in a new era and India was on the march again.

The nature of the movement may be described in the words of the great French writer, Romain Rolland. He says:

"For more than thirty centuries the tree of vision with all its thousand branches and their million twigs, has sprung from that torrid land, the burning womb of the gods. It renews itself tirelessly, showing no signs of decay, all kinds of fruits ripen on its boughs at the same time; side by side are found all kinds of gods from the most savage to the highest—to the formless God, the unnameable, the boundless one...always the same true."

The British impact was like the application of hoe and shears to prune the rotten roots and the dead branches. For India it was like the advent of the spring tide after the inhibitory hiberanatism of a formidable winter. The destruction wrought by British rulers to the polity and economy of India and the consequential changes of this destruction have been mentioned above. It is not necessary to reiterate that those changes though in some cases quite radical, failed to effect a social revolution which could only take place if Indian economy had grown out of its medieval agrarian system into a modern industrial regime. Whatever degree of modernisation was achieved was more or less confined to the cities and affected the villages only indirectly and superficially.

The change of mind was largely a bourgeoisie phenomenon, a change of the middle class intelligentsia. This was natural and inevitable. The educated class alone had the opportunity to assimilate western knowledge, to study closely western science, philosophy and literature and to learn by actual participation in western type activities—personal and public, the values and modes of western life. Their reaction to the new ideology from the West took several forms. Some Indians were swept off their feet completely, they rejected their Indian traditions root and branch and in Macaulay's words were Indians only in colour but in everything else—in thought and sentiment, English. A second school of thought took the opposite extreme and justified the whole of this tradition—including the myths, superstitions and good and evil practices. In the middle was a group of thinkers who endeavoured to sift the wheat from the chaff, the rational and the pure and the high-minded from the fatuous, degrading and false.

The first group made its debut as Young Bengal and consisted largely of the alumni of the recently opened Hindu College and their admirers. Derozio, the young English teacher was the inspirer of their intellectual freedom. The second group followed Raja Radha Kant Deb and his Dharma Sabha, a society of conservatives. The pioneer of the third school was Ram Mohan Roy, the father of modern India.

Among the Muslims there were similar developments, though their appearance was not simultaneous with the Hindu movements. Shah Wali Ullah of Delhi was a revivalist thinker and a conservative reformer who lived in the latter part of the 18th century. His school became the centre of a widespread propaganda drive against the cultural and political domination of the West. The so-called Wahabi uprising which caused a considerable strain on the Government of India's financial and military resources and for over 40 years kept law and order in the northern provinces of India in a disturbed state, was an offshoot of the school. A number of Maulvis trained under its auspices took prominent part in the Revolt of 1857 and after its suppression founded the Deoband Madrasa whose teachers and pupils were among the foremost fighters in the Indian struggle for freedom.

Sir Syed Ahmad was a reformer who was greatly influenced by western thought. He founded the M.A.O. College to educate

Muslim youth in modernised Islamic theology and western scientific knowledge. Syed Amir Ali was a rationalist who wrote extensively on Islamic religion, history and culture and presented Islam as a tolerant, progressive and enlightened faith.

The traditionists who refused to apply critical and rational methods to the study of Islam, because they held it to be a revealed religion, worked to remove the innovations which had crept into beliefs and practices and to restore the pristine purity of the faith.

Obviously Hindu and Muslim India was stirred to its depths by the impact of the West. The result was a transformation in the spirit of Indian culture which manifested itself in art, literature, outlook upon life and the world and motive of conduct—of the individual and society, as also in ways of living and manners and customs.

But as pointed out above the fundamental change consisted in the emergence of the new man. The individual who took reason for authority and even when he accepted the authority of the scriptures and revered the texts which provided regulations for his conduct as divinely ordained, he did so after a process of enquiry and argument. Thus the challenge of the West awakened the faculties of the individual which had remained inert or dormant. Suddenly the world which was illusory, unreal, the place of suffering and sorrow had become real, the theatre of struggle, triumph and joy. No longer was helpless man the play-thing of an unknown destiny, but an independent agent seeking to attain mastery over human and natural forces.

The Indians who contributed towards this revolution were many. But I have time to name only a few—Raja Ram Mohan Roy, Syed Ahmad Khan, Swami Dayanand Saraswati, Ram Knohna Paramhans, Rabindra Nath Tagore, and Mohandas Karamchand Gandhi.

Ram Mohan Roy was a man of massive intellect and infinite courage. In the depressing atmosphere of the early nineteenth century when the Christian missionaries and the British officials were pouring contempt on Indian civilisation and denigrating Indian religions, he rebuked the missionaries by leading a counter attack upon their dogmas and based it upon a close and critical study of the Christian scriptures and books of theology in the Hebrew, Greek, Latin and English languages. He affirmed the faith of the Hindus on the sole and sufficient foundation of the Upanishads which he translated from Sanskrit into Bengali and English. He called upon his countrymen to discard blind faith and to trust to their individual judgment and inner light.

Syed Ahmad Khan (1818-98) was a younger contemporary of Ram Mohan Roy. He belonged to an aristocratic family of Delhi which was attached to the court of the Mughal emperors. The ruination of the empire obliged him to take service under the new rulers of India, and the contact with the British made him realise the inwardness of the decay of Muslim society, and the secret of the strength of the British people. He saw how disregard of reason and science had led to superstition, moral corruption and degradation. He resolved to purify Islam of its excrescences, to demonstrate that its teachings were wholly rational and in complete agreement with the laws of nature. He urged his community to abandon its irrational approach to religion, abjure the evil customs which vitiated and enervated society and adopt western progressive ideas without losing the hold upon the original and pure form of this faith. His indomitable courage, unfaltering perseverance and dominating personality triumphed over the hostility of his shortsighted correligionists and succeeded in instilling a new vitality in the community.

Dayanand Saraswati was a sturdy fighter against all superstitions, against polytheism and caste. His appeal was directed not so much towards the sophisticated anglicised Indian aristocrat as towards the middle class intelligentsia of Northern India. His movement had an electric effect, similar to that of Calvin and John Knox, in stimulating puritanical attitudes towards life and social affairs, and in vitalising the self-respect of man.

Rama Krishna was a mystic, who had dedicated himself to the service of God-Mother. He saw in every man the image of God and therefore advocated "not mercy, but service, service, for man must be regarded as God." In communion with living, loving, suffering humanity he found the highest form of self-fulfilment.

Tagore was a revolutionary poet and seer. For India which was oppressed with the heavy burden of Weltschmerz in his soul which tormented herself by intensifying life with suffering and pains, and was bound in chains which bruised his spirit, he brought the message of love, joy and freedom. But in his case it is best to give the taste of his thought in his own inimitable words. Of the beauty and joy of nature and her identity with the divine he says:

> Thou art the sky, and thou art the nest as well.
> O! Thou Beautiful, there in the nest it is thy love that encloses the soul with colours and sounds and odour.
> There comes the morning, with the golden basket in her right hand, bearing the wreath of beauty, silently to the earth.
>
> And there comes the evening over the lonely meadows deserted by herds through trackless paths, carrying cool draughts of peace in her golden pitcher from the Western ocean of rest.
>
> But there, where spreads the Infinite sky, for the soul to take her flight in, reigns the stainless white radiance. There is no day nor night, nor form, nor colour, and never, never, a word.

And the freedom of which he dreams is:

> Where the mind is without fear and the head is held high:
> Where knowledge is free:
> Where the world has not been broken up into fragments by narrow domestic walls:
> Where words come out from the depth of truth:

Where tireless striving stretches its arms towards perfection:

Where the clear stream of reason has not lost its way into the dreary desert sand of dead habit:

Where the mind is led forward by Thee into ever widening thought and action:

Into that heaven of freedom, my Father let my country awake.

Gandhi strove to translate India's vision into the practice of society. He showed how the discipline of yoga was not only a pre-requisite for the enlightenment of the soul, but equally a preparation for liberation from the irrational strivings of the self and for the attainment of freedom from bondage to the other. For him non-violence was the law of life and truth the lodestar for the guidance of human conduct. Both non-violence and truth are inherent in the higher reason of man. He was the exemplar of the ideal man—the man who lives in society by reasoned action.

As time passes and the new vision pervades the country this onesidedness which dominated the mind and manifested itself in social disintegration in the form of communalism, casteism, and particularism of various sorts will be dispelled. Then the new man will spring into life—the integrated man, the free man, the universal man, the man whose stream of consciousness (**mana**) will flow between the unmoving banks of self-consciousness (**atman**) through its length to the ocean of life universal and eternal.

It will pass through the eddies and whirlpools of the transient world disciplined and directed by the abiding guides—the stern, silent sentinel who stands by the side. Then will the truth of the individual be vindicated and he will shine forth in his real glory. Then will the stage be reached when the caravan of humanity having traversed its long and exciting journey will forge forward to climb heights of unforeseen possibilities and unlimited promise.